Mary Berry is known to millions through her fortnightly cookery spot on Thames Television's magazine programme, *After Noon Plus*. She is a regular contributor to BBC's *Woman's Hour* and often takes part in BBC and local radio phone-in programmes.

Mary Berry was, for several years, cookery editor of *Ideal Home* and is now the freezer consultant for *Family Circle*. She is one of Britain's most popular cookery writers and has written over twenty books.

1 lb mince
1 onion
2 Stock Cubes
1 tsp Mixed Herbs.   ½ hr
    15 oz Tin Tomatoes
        Salt
    5 oz Water.

    8 oz SR Flour
    4 oz Marg.
        Salt.   + Chill
    ¼ Pint Water
    200°   20 mins

Also by Mary Berry in Sphere Books:

FAST CAKES
FRUIT FARE
FAST STARTERS, SOUPS AND SALADS
FAST SUPPERS
FAST DESSERTS
NEW FREEZER COOKBOOK
KITCHEN WISDOM

Feed Your Family the Healthier Way

MARY BERRY

SPHERE BOOKS LIMITED

First published in Great Britain by
Judy Piatkus (Publishers) Limited 1985
Copyright © 1985 Mary Berry
Published by Sphere Books Ltd 1986
27 Wright's Lane, London W8 5SW

Author's Acknowledgment

This indeed has been an interesting book to write – and without
Debbie Woolhead it would not have been such fun. Debbie
has helped to test and develop these recipes, always taking such
care to make them taste and look good as well as being
extremely healthy.

Printed and bound in Great Britain by
Collins, Glasgow

CONTENTS

INTRODUCTION

Family meal times are a very important part of my life. Whether we are rushing through breakfast or, by supper time, swapping stories of our day in a more leisurely way, any meal is a valuable time when the family are gathered together. So when I first began thinking about the newest views on healthy eating, my first concern was to find out whether they could lead to really good recipes? Dishes I worked out had to pass the family test – to be as good as, or better than, the dishes we already enjoyed together.

This book is the result of what I discovered. It is a book of family recipes which incorporate the latest thinking on sensible, healthier eating. It isn't intended to be a wholefood book – full of recipes for peas, beans, lentils and free-range eggs – nor is it intended to be the *ultimate* word in healthy eating. For one thing, worthy brown dishes constantly served to my family would cause a riot; for another, I believe you must approach new ideas gradually. Once the family have got accustomed to the proportion I recommend of, say, wholewheat flour in a crumble topping or pie pastry, you can *up* that quantity, until you may be able to cut out white flour altogether. Cut down *gradually*, too, on the quantities of salt and sugar, until you are happy with a new, healthy balance.

My way, over the past few years, has been to aim to feed the family on more interesting, healthier food. I have pin-pointed a number of ways of achieving this – by eating more of certain things, by cutting down on others – and I list them for you below. Together they add up to a new, more sensible and healthier way of eating.

Eat More 'Real' Food

This is the basis of my approach to the modern, more healthy eating – go for what is 'real'. Sadly, much of the food manufactured today has been refined, processed and added to, thus often completely negating many of the original nutritional properties of the food.

Real foods are fresh and unadulterated – vegetables, fruits, fish and lean meat plus grains – with as few refinements as possible, and they should then be prepared and cooked in as healthy a way as possible. Many commercial packeted, freeze-dried, bottled, canned and frozen

7

foods have got additives, preservatives, colouring, flavouring, etc *added* to them, which may make them look better, taste better and last better, but they're not *real*, nor are they very good for you.

Real foods contain *all* the nutrients required by the body – protein, carbohydrate, fat, dietary fibre, minerals, vitamins and fluid. Careful selection, buying, preparation and cooking will ensure that the whole family will benefit.

Eat More Dietary Fibre

Much has been written about this recently, and there have been several best-selling books on the subject – bearing out fibre's importance in the diet. Fibre is the cellulose which is the principal structure of grains, vegetable and fruit (including also the husk, skin and peel). As we cannot digest this, it acts to remove waste products speedily from the body, and some such food should be served at every meal. It is a major disease preventative, and there is *no* fibre in meat, fish, eggs, cheese, butter, milk or sugar, which make up the bulk of the present Western diet.

The refined foods that are sold nowadays have had much of their original nutritive values and dietary fibre stripped from them, some for mere cosmetic value, some because, refined, they *keep* better on the supermarket shelf. Flour and flour products such as bread and pasta, as well as rice, are prime examples of this. They have been refined (as well as added to), and as a result they are less rich in natural dietary fibre than their 'brown' equivalents – wholemeal or wholewheat flour, wholemeal or wholewheat bread, wholemeal pasta and brown rice.

Change Over to Brown Gradually

You can work on the idea that natural foods add an extra element of interest, for a more positive approach. When I started my family on brown rice, for instance, they found it a bit chewy (it's the whole rice grain, nothing removed). So I went at it a bit more slowly. Next time, I mixed brown with American long-grain white rice and the family loved it. As time has gone by I have decreased the white rice and now they *love* brown – especially in salads, by the way. (I still serve white rice with curry, though, just because it goes best with it!)

Wholemeal flour (sometimes called wholewheat) is the whole grain of wheat ground down into flour. If you buy white flour, this has been produced by removing the tiny wheatgerm from each grain (the most nutritious part) as well as the bran (the fibre). Wheatmeal has had about half the bran and wheatgerm removed. 100% wholemeal and wholewheat have nothing removed from them, so these (the names are interchangeable) are the flours and the breads to choose. My way is to remember the word *whole*, meaning the whole grain with nothing left out.

I would advise everyone to use wholemeal flour and brown bread whenever possible, every day, in preference to white. Again, do this gradually if the family is accustomed to white bread. We haven't cut it out by any means; I still serve hamburgers, for instance, in fresh white baps (buns), and the family enjoy crusty French sticks on occasions. But if you ensure that brown bread is always available, you will soon find that its hunger-satisfying qualities make it the first choice when a 'starving' child rushes in for a piece of bread and butter! You will notice that I specify a proportion of wholemeal flour in many of my recipes. Increase the proportion of wholemeal gradually, if feasible, for even healthier meals.

If you've tried wholewheat pasta, you will have found, like my family, that it has more taste than the usual 'white' sort. It is also, because of the wholewheat flour used instead of strong white flour, much richer in dietary fibre. I can recommend wholewheat tagliatelle, and sometimes serve a mixture of this with the white or green type (the colour comes from spinach, incidentally). It looks very effective, which is especially important once you start serving more 'whole' foods. I am very careful to add lots of colour – tomato, carrot or bright green vegetables – to dishes so they don't ever look too worthy or too brown!

Eat More Vegetables and Fruit

These are 'real' foods *par excellence*, and should be served at every meal if possible. They are also major sources of dietary fibre as well as of vitamins and minerals.

Vegetables should be bought carefully and served raw, or cooked very briefly. Green leafy vegetables, which have the highest content of Vitamin C, for instance, taste far better raw or cooked lightly anyway – cabbage, spinach and sprouts have a fresh taste which is worlds removed from the truly dreadful 'schoolday' smell of overcooked greens. I am sure we are better vegetable cooks already than our grandmothers who boiled green vegetables 'to death', for not only did the vegetables lose flavour and texture, but also all their vitamins, thrown away with the cooking liquid. Steam vegetables if you can (see the vegetable chapter), and use all cooking water for stocks, soups and sauces.

Don't trim away too much from your vegetables, either. Often the outside leaves of cabbage are the greenest, the most full of goodness. Wash well and cut out any discoloured bits. My family now enjoy potatoes in their skins, both jacket-baked and boiled. The most nutritious part in the potato is in a layer just under the skin – as with *most* vegetables in fact – so when you peel you are discarding all that goodness and flavour. Scrub vegetables well instead.

But I don't advise you ever to fall into the trap of displaying your knowledge. I never tell the family to 'eat up your greens, they're good for you'. It just doesn't sound very enticing, does it? Serve without comment: the children will notice for themselves that potatoes or sprouts just taste more interesting when cooked in the ways I recommend.

I aim to grow as many vegetables as possible myself, or buy local fresh ones in season. I can then be *sure* that they're really fresh, as fresh-picked vegetables retain the most flavour. (Pick-your-own farms are also an excellent source.) Supermarket vegetables have improved greatly and I find those sold in Marks and Spencer lead the way for being in peak condition – a result of wise buying and rapid turnover. Don't ever buy wilted or tired looking vegetables for your family – no amount of clever cooking can restore the flavour.

While on the subject of vegetables, dried pulses like peas, beans and lentils are valuable in the diet. They no longer contain the Vitamin C of the fresh bean or pea (although sprouted, they contain *more*, interestingly), but they are full of fibre, vegetable protein and good filling carbohydrate. Other advantages are that they store well on the larder shelf, to use when food supplies are running short mid-week. All need to be soaked overnight in cold water (if not using straightaway, they can be kept in the fridge another 24 hours) before being cooked until just tender in fresh boiling water. To avoid the dreadfully dull colour of many bean dishes it is vital not to mix the dark ones like red kidney or aduki beans with pale ones such as haricots. While cooking the colour runs into the pale beans and make the whole dish a sludgy brown. Mix after cooking.

Fresh fruit, too, should form a major daily part of your family's diet. One orange holds a daily dose of Vitamin C, and an apple a day, as everyone knows, 'keeps the doctor away' – (because of the vitamins and the fibre in the skin: *never* peel fruit like apples). Fruit can be a breakfast, a snack, or a pudding, *much* healthier than a sweetened commercial cereal, a biscuit, or jam roll. Dried fruits, too, although lacking the Vitamin C of fresh, are good for the family.

Cut Down on Fats

The body *needs* a certain amount of fat, but not in the quantity we are now eating. For fats are not only obvious – the fat on meat, the oil or dripping used in cooking, for instance – but are also hidden. Meat and fish *flesh* contain fat, as do butter, cheese and milk.

Saturated or animal fats can cause a build-up of cholesterol in the arteries, leading to a variety of diseases. Unsaturated fats are better to use than saturated – the vegetable oils such as safflower, corn and sunflower, as well as the natural oils of seeds and nuts – but less fat of *whatever* kind ought to be eaten. Fish contains on the whole more unsaturated than saturated fat; meat the opposite.

Many of these facts will be familiar to readers from slimming diets. My aim – and that of the modern ideas on eating – is to introduce them into everyday family eating too. To cut down may sound technical or difficult, but by following my tips and recipes, it can be easy as well as tasty!

The leanest meats are chicken and turkey. If I choose beef or lamb, I always trim excess fat off before it is cooked. In many recipes I cook by the healthiest methods – grilling (broiling) for instance. And if something does require frying, I tend to use a non-stick pan (skillet) so that the merest trace of oil is needed. Start minced (ground) beef, too, over a gentle heat in a non-stick pan (skillet), and when the natural fat begins to run out, you can increase the heat and fry as usual (you might even be able to spoon *out* some fat).

And also beware of the less obvious fats. Use polyunsaturated margarines instead of butter in cooking (although sometimes butter is vital for its flavour), skimmed milk and low-fat cheeses. Remember that sauces and gravies contain fats – from the dripping, butter or cream used. Make up vegetable purées and use them instead of sauces to enhance a piece of grilled chicken, say, if it seems dry, and try low-fat natural yogurt as a cream alternative, either *in* a sauce, or as a topping.

Cut Down on Sugar and Salt

Both sugar and salt should be cut down considerably in the new healthy eating.

White refined sugar is neither good for the teeth nor the figure – it consists of calories only, with no nutrients whatsoever. We as a family certainly eat a good deal less sugar at home. In fact, the sugars I do keep are chiefly golden granulated and the unrefined sugars – which can claim to have a little more going for them. They are also so much more interesting to spoon on to porridge or yogurt, with their treacly taste. Honey, too, is a marvellous sweetener, and can often be added to cold fruits and the desserts already in your cooking repertoire, instead of sugar. These unrefined sugars and honey taste better, to my mind, because they have their own natural sweetness and flavour. They are more 'real'. Their usage, though, should still be limited to a certain extent, and remember that a great many manufactured foods like breakfast cereals and fruit yogurts contain a lot of sugar.

Salt and its valuable versus damaging properties, is being debated at

11

the moment. Sodium chloride – salt – is needed by the body, but a regular high salt intake is believed to contribute to high blood pressure amongst other things. Never *add* salt at the table: in fact, I recommend that you tell your family to rely on your judgement of seasoning in the dish, and don't allow the salt cellar on the table. Cut down too on foods with a high sodium content – ham, bacon, potato crisps, salted nuts, processed food in general.

Do switch to healthier family eating. It is well worth it. As you will see from the recipes, I have not gone overboard on the principles I have just outlined, but have, I hope, given you recipes that will start you and your family on a healthier track. It is perfectly possible still to serve some of the familiar rich and wicked dishes that the family enjoy, by balancing the day's meals or the week's meals as a whole – and merely by including more of the fibre foods like cereals, vegetables, brown breads and so on, you will find their satisfying properties so effective that the family will not *need* to 'fill up' with sugary or fatty foods. As time goes by, you will find that their taste for them decreases anyway.

So now, straight on to the recipes – and here's to your very good health!

BREAKFAST – OFF TO A GOOD START

I have had to tempt the children back to having breakfast during the week. For ages none of us have felt we wanted, or could spare the time, to cook and eat the big traditional British fried breakfast every day. And anyway, both eggs and bacon, although delicious, can be less than healthy: egg yolks are high in cholesterol and need fat for frying; and bacon contains a lot of sodium which you should not serve too much of.

The Continental breakfast, too, does not fare any better in the light of modern ideas on healthy eating. Black coffee has no food value, and croissants are very high in fat and calories – as of course are the butter and jams you put on them – and leave you hungry again in no time.

The body *needs* a good input in the morning after a night's fast, and especially *growing* bodies. Children going to school need protein, vitamins, fibre, fluid and the energy supplied by carbohydrates and a moderate amount of fat. Adults, too, need a good nutritional start to the day.

Milk and milk products such as yogurt, selected cereals (many commercial varieties are high in sugar and additives: read the labels), fruit and fruit juices, a moderate amount of protein (such as fish, a boiled or poached egg, a little grilled [broiled] or baked meat) are the prime requirements, and the recipes on the following pages should give you some basics upon which you can ring the healthy changes.

Special Home-Made Muesli

This is what I consider the best answer to the breakfast problem: home-made muesli. (Bought varieties often contain a high proportion of sugar – and it is cheaper and much better to make your own.) The children find my muesli is acceptably fast to spoon out and eat before the rush to school or to a friend's house for the day. It is an excellent source of fibre with its mixture of grains, fruit and nuts. We all love it. I make up a supply about every 10 days and vary it each time so as to avoid 'sameness'. Sometimes I add snipped dried apricots or a few sunflower seeds to the mixture. When serving I add perhaps a few raspberries or small strawberries to each plate, or slice a banana up to add to the flavour.

Most ingredients should now be available in good supermarkets, but if not, you'll find them in health-food shops.

Imperial/metric	American
4 oz (100 g) rolled oats	1 cup rolled oats
2 oz (50 g) wheatgerm	½ cup wheatgerm
2 oz (50 g) bran	½ cup bran
1 oz (25 g) hazelnuts, chopped	¼ cup filberts, chopped
2 oz (50 g) sultanas	⅓ cup seedless white raisins
2 oz (50 g) raisins, chopped	⅓ cup raisins, chopped
2 oz (50 g) dried apple, chopped	½ cup dried apple, chopped
1 oz (25 g) sesame seeds	1 tablespoon sesame seeds

Mix all the ingredients together in a bowl and store in a lidded plastic container until required.

Serve in a bowl with cold milk, a fruit such as sliced apple or banana, and a sprinkling of demerara (Turbinado) sugar (it shouldn't *really* need sugar).

Breakfast Fruits

Fruit is one of the major sources of both Vitamin C and fibre, and this exotic mix makes for a very refreshing breakfast.

Imperial/metric	American
1 ripe pawpaw (papaya)	*1 ripe pawpaw*
1 ripe mango	*1 ripe mango*
1 kiwi fruit	*1 kiwi*
juice of 1 lemon	*juice of 1 lemon*

First prepare the fruits. Peel, seed and slice the pawpaw. Peel the mango, remove the stone and slice. Peel and slice the kiwi fruit. Arrange the fruits on serving plates and sprinkle with lemon juice. Chill well in the refrigerator before serving.

Serves 4

Grapefruit and Orange

Again, this is an excellent source of fibre and Vitamin C in particular. When in season stir in a few fresh cherries.

Imperial/metric	American
2 grapefruit	*2 grapefruit*
2 large Jaffa oranges	*2 large sweet oranges*

Peel and segment the grapefruit and oranges. To do this start by peeling the fruits then remove all pith, hold the fruit in one hand and with a sharp knife dissect out each segment, leaving the membrane and skin behind. Mix both fruits together in a bowl, cover with clingfilm (plastic wrap) and chill in the refrigerator overnight before serving, in tall stemmed glasses.

Serves 3

Winter Fruit Compote

Buy dried fruits from good supermarkets or health-food shops. They are rich in potassium, if not in the Vitamin C of the fresh, and can be a valuable addition to anyone's diet. Watch out for sun-dried particularly.

If you buy a quantity and your store cupboard is warm, then store in polythene (plastic) bags in the freezer either soaked or unsoaked. Label clearly. Serve the compote chilled on its own, or with natural (unflavoured) yogurt (see next recipe for home-made).

Imperial/metric	American
2 oz (50 g) dried figs	⅓ cup dried figs
2 oz (50 g) dried apricots	⅓ cup dried apricots
2 oz (50 g) dried peaches	⅓ cup dried peaches
2 oz (50 g) dried prunes	⅓ cup dried prunes
2 oz (50 g) dried apple rings	⅓ cup dried apple rings
2 oz (50 g) sultanas	⅓ cup seedless white raisins
¾ pint (450 ml) water	scant 2 cups water
4 oz (100 g) light muscovado sugar (or less, to taste)	½ cup firmly packed light brown sugar
1 strip lemon rind	1 strip lemon rind
1 teaspoon ground nutmeg	1 teaspoon ground nutmeg
1 teaspoon ground cinnamon	1 teaspoon ground cinnamon

Put all the fruits in a bowl with the water and leave to stand overnight.

Next day, strain off water into a pan, and add the sugar, lemon rind and spices. Simmer gently for 10 minutes then add the fruit. Cover with a lid and continue to simmer for about an hour until the fruit is tender. Remove and discard the lemon rind and leave to cool.

Serves 4 to 6

Home-Made Yogurt

Yogurt is a good breakfast food. It contains B vitamins, and more A and D than the milk from which it was made. It also contains good bacteria which help digestion. Keep it in the fridge for adding to breakfast cereals, for topping fruit and a variety of puddings, and for stirring into sauces.

Use your own home-made yogurt for up to three times as a culture, then start again using a bought one.

Imperial/metric	American
1 pint (600 ml) milk	2½ cups milk
2 heaped teaspoons bought natural yogurt (the culture)	2 heaped teaspoons unflavored yogurt
1 heaped tablespoon dried milk powder	1 heaped tablespoon dried milk powder

Heat the milk in a pan to boiling point, then cool in a bowl of cold water to about 60°C/112°F – the temperature of a hot bath! Put the yogurt in a bowl with the milk and whisk in the milk powder.

Cover and put either in a warm cupboard for about 12 hours or in a wide-mouthed vacuum flask for about 6 hours. (You could also use a commercial yogurt-making 'machine'; follow the manufacturer's instructions.)

Store yogurt in the fridge when cool.

Makes 1 pint/600 ml (2¼ cups)

Flavoured Yogurts

Flavouring your own home-made yogurts can be fun and they taste so much fresher than those which are flavoured commercially. The addition of fruit and/or nuts or a little muesli adds to the fibre and vitamin content.

A basic 5 oz/150g (⅔ cup) of natural plain yogurt can be mixed with any of the following, then well chilled.

HONEY AND HAZELNUT (FILBERT)

Imperial/metric	American
1 tablespoon runny honey	1 tablespoon clear honey
1 oz (25 g) sultanas	1 tablespoon seedless white raisins
1 oz (25 g) hazelnuts, chopped	1 tablespoon filberts, chopped

RASPBERRY

Imperial/metric	American
2 oz (50 g) fresh raspberries	⅓ cup raspberries
1 oz (25 g) golden granulated sugar	2 tablespoons sugar

BANANA

Imperial/metric	American
1 small banana, sliced	1 small banana, sliced
a little demerara sugar, sprinkled on top	a little Turbinado sugar, sprinkled on top

APPLE AND SULTANA

Imperial/metric	American
1 Cox's apple, cored and sliced	1 dessert apple, cored and sliced
1 oz (25 g) sultanas	1 tablespoon white seedless raisins

Family Oven Grill

If there are several family and friends for breakfast I find it a good idea –
and much easier! – to cook the breakfast in the oven in individual dishes.
I use round shallow Le Creuset dishes. The baking process is basically
much healthier than frying.

Imperial/metric	American
4 sausages	4 large pork sausage links
4 rashers back bacon, derinded and trimmed of fat	4 Canadian bacon slices
4 eggs	4 eggs
4 tomatoes, halved	4 tomatoes, halved

Prick the sausages with a fork and arrange in four individual ovenproof
dishes or a roasting tin. Cook in the oven at 400°F/200°C/Gas 6 for about
10 minutes until the fat has begun to run out, then add the bacon and
return to the oven for 5 more minutes. Spoon out most of the fat from
each dish, then break the eggs into the dishes and add the tomatoes, cut
side down. Return to the oven for about 10 minutes until the egg has
cooked and the bacon is crispy.

Serve straight from the oven in the individual dishes or if the breakfast
has been cooked in a tin, serve on warmed plates.

Serves 4

Poached Eggs with Brown Muffins

Muffins are readily available in most supermarkets and bakers, wholemeal (wholewheat) ones are particularly nice – and much healthier. Or you could try using the granary rolls or wholewheat scones on pages 170 and 171.

Imperial/metric	American
4 wholemeal muffins	4 wholewheat muffins
4 eggs	4 eggs
4 rashers back bacon	4 Canadian bacon slices
2 tomatoes, halved	2 tomatoes, cut in half

Split each muffin in half. Poach the eggs in boiling salted water for about 5 minutes, then drain well. Grill (broil) the bacon until crispy, and the tomatoes until cooked. Toast the muffins on both sides, then serve each person with two pieces of muffin, a poached egg on one half and bacon and tomato on the other half.

Serves 4

Scottish Herrings

Herrings are an oily fish, but the protein and vitamin content, as well as the fat content, are necessary in a healthy diet. Serve them garnished with wedges of lemon and a sprig of fresh parsley.

Imperial/metric	American
4 herrings, filleted	4 herrings, cleaned and filleted
2 oz (50 g) porridge oats	½ cup rolled oats
a dash of dried mustard	a little dried mustard
a little sunflower oil	a little sunflower oil

Wash the herrings, dry them thoroughly on kitchen paper towels, and open flat. Mix the oats with the mustard and thoroughly coat the herrings. Heat the oil in a frying pan (skillet) and fry the fish until golden brown on both sides, turning once during cooking. They will take about 10 minutes. Drain well on kitchen paper towels, arrange on a serving dish and serve hot.

Serves 4

Jugged Kippers

Kippers too are oily, but delicious to serve at breakfast. By 'cooking' in this traditional way, you need use no extra fat, and there's no smell.

Imperial/metric	American
2 kipper fillets	2 kipper fillets
boiling water	boiling water

Put the kipper fillets in a jug or shallow dish. Pour boiling water over them so that they are completely covered with water. Cover the jug or dish with a plate or piece of foil. Leave without any further heating for 5 minutes. Drain off the water and the kippers will be cooked to perfection. Transfer to a serving plate and serve warm.

Serves 2

Kedgeree

The brown rice gives this dish a lovely nutty flavour, as well as additional fibre. The fish gives protein as do the eggs. Use less butter if you like, or a polyunsaturated margarine.

Imperial/metric	American
3 oz (75 g) brown rice	½ cup brown rice
salt	salt
3 oz (75 g) long-grain rice	½ cup long-grain rice
2 hard-boiled eggs	2 hard-cooked eggs
12 oz (350 g) smoked haddock fillets	12 oz smoked haddock fillets
2 oz (50 g) butter	¼ cup butter
juice of ½ lemon	juice of ½ lemon
salt	salt
cayenne pepper	cayenne pepper
sprigs of parsley to garnish	sprigs of parsley to garnish

Cook the two rices separately (because of the different cooking times) in plenty of boiling salted water as directed on the packet. Rinse well, drain, and keep warm. Cut a few slices of egg for garnish and reserve; roughly chop the remainder.

Poach the smoked haddock in a little water for about 10 minutes. Drain and remove all skin and any bones, then flake the fish.

Melt the butter in a large pan, add the rice, eggs and fish and heat through slowly: stir in the lemon juice, and add salt and cayenne pepper to taste. Pile into a warmed dish and serve garnished with sprigs of parsley and slices of egg.

Serves 4

TO BEGIN WITH

I discovered some years ago that if I gave the family a starter, they were replete by the end of the main course, and far less likely to ask hopefully whether there was a sweet pudding to follow! So serving a first course can help in the battle for healthier eating.

And for health, think mainly in terms of fruit and vegetables, and good home-made vegetable soups. At least then you can be sure, particularly with fussy children, that they have taken in the vegetable and fruit goodness, when they are hungry, before the main course when they may turn their noses up at the accompanying vegetables. Take a look, too, at the vegetable and salad sections: many of the recipes there could be adapted to serve as a starter.

Most of the first courses here are ones you can prepare ahead. When you choose one, consider the courses that follow so that the texture, colour and flavours will contrast. The simple rule is – don't repeat yourself. A common fault is to have a fruity first course, then finish with fresh fruit, say, or summer pudding! The repetition is boring to the palate, however delicious each individual course.

In this section, too, I have included a few 'snacks'. So often these days, as life gets busier, a meal has to be quick – and by applying many of the new healthier eating ideas, a snack can be a perfectly healthy meal.

Tomato and Avocado

This is a colourful starter, lovely to serve on a hot summer's day. The avocado is one of the most nutritious fruits (if not one of the most slimming, due to its natural oils), and tomatoes are high in Vitamin C.

Imperial/metric	American
4 tomatoes	4 tomatoes
2 ripe avocado pears	2 ripe avocado pears
juice of ½ lemon	juice ½ lemon
4 tablespoons French dressing (see page 134)	4 tablespoons French dressing (see page 134)
1 tablespoon freshly chopped chives	1 tablespoon freshly chopped chives

Slice the tomatoes and arrange each attractively on four individual dishes. Cut the avocado pears in half, remove the stones, peel and slice. Dip the slices of avocado in the lemon juice to prevent them from discolouring, then arrange on top of tomato. Pour a little French dressing on top and sprinkle with chopped chives.

Serve really well chilled.

Serves 4

Piquant Pears with Prawns (Shelled Shrimp)

Avocado pears are always a favourite first course in our house, and this is a particularly nice way of serving them. They are rich in vitamins and minerals, and the prawns add non-fattening protein.

Imperial/metric	American
3 ripe avocado pears	3 ripe avocado pears
2 good tablespoons mayonnaise (see page 132)	2 tablespoons mayonnaise (see page 132)
2 tablespoons natural yogurt (see page 17)	2 tablespoons unflavored yogurt (see page 17)
1 tablespoon tomato ketchup	1 tablespoon tomato catsup
1 tablespoon horseradish cream	1 tablespoon horseradish cream
Worcestershire sauce	Worcestershire sauce
juice of ½ lemon	juice of ½ lemon
8 oz (225 g) peeled prawns	1⅓ cups shelled shrimp
paprika pepper	paprika pepper

Chill the avocados in the refrigerator for about an hour before you serve them.

Measure the mayonnaise, yogurt, ketchup, horseradish cream, a few drops of Worcestershire sauce and the lemon juice into a bowl, and mix thoroughly. Stir in the prawns and chill in the refrigerator, covered with clingfilm (plastic wrap).

To serve, cut the avocados in half, remove the stones, and brush the flesh with a little extra lemon juice to prevent them from discolouring. Arrange on serving dishes. Taste and check seasoning of the prawn filling then spoon into the centre of the pears. Sprinkle with a little paprika pepper and serve.

Serves 6

Melon and Prawns (Shelled Shrimp)

This is a deliciously light first course, combining Vitamin C and protein. Serve in the melon skins, garnished with wedges of lemon and watercress sprigs.

Imperial/metric

1 Honeydew melon
8 oz (225 g) prawns

Sauce

¼ pint (150 ml) natural yogurt (see page 17)
¼ pint (150 ml) mayonnaise (see page 132)
3 teaspoons horseradish cream
2 teaspoons Worcestershire sauce
2 tablespoons tomato ketchup
salt and freshly ground black pepper
lemon wedges and sprigs of watercress to garnish

American

1 Honeydew melon
1⅓ cups shelled shrimp

Sauce

⅔ cup unflavored yogurt (see page 17)
⅔ cup mayonnaise (see page 132)
3 teaspoons horseradish cream
2 teaspoons Worcestershire sauce
2 tablespoons tomato catsup
salt and freshly ground black pepper
lemon wedges and sprigs watercress to garnish

Divide the melon into six segments. Remove and discard the seeds, cut the flesh from the skins, then cube it. Drain the melon and prawns well on kitchen paper towels.

For the sauce blend all the ingredients together and season to taste. Just before serving mix the melon and prawns with the sauce.

Arrange the melon skins on serving dishes then spoon the melon mixture on top. Garnish with sprigs of watercress and lemon wedges, and serve immediately.

Serves 6

Tropical Melon

Melon is a light and very slimming starter (it contains so much water!), and you can cut down on the syrup content if you like.

Serve really well chilled in tall stemmed individual glasses, decorated with a sprig of mint.

Imperial/metric

1 Honeydew melon
15 oz (425 g) can lychees in
   natural syrup
3 oz (75 g) stem ginger, roughly
   chopped
1 kiwi fruit, peeled and sliced

American

1 Honeydew melon
2 cups canned litchis
⅓ cup preserved ginger, roughly
   chopped
1 kiwi, peeled and sliced

Cut the melon in half, scoop out and discard the seeds, then cut the flesh into cubes (or use a baller to give balls of melon). Put melon in a bowl with the contents of the can of lychees, cover with clingfilm (plastic wrap) and chill in the refrigerator overnight.

Just before serving stir in the ginger and kiwi fruit and divide between glasses to serve.

Serves 6

Hors d'Oeuvres

Arrange the hors d'oeuvres on individual plates for a really healthy and colourful first course. I sometimes increase the portions and serve it for lunch.

Imperial/metric	American
6 small eggs (size 6), hard-boiled	6 small eggs, hard-cooked
¼ pint (150 ml) good mayonnaise (see page 132)	⅔ cup good mayonnaise (see page 132)
2 oz (56 g) can anchovy fillets in oil, drained	¼ cup anchovy fillets, drained
⅓ pint (200 ml) French dressing (see page 134)	1 cup French dressing (see page 134)
1 very small iceburg lettuce, finely shredded	1 very small crisphead or iceburg lettuce, finely shredded
1 tablespoon freshly chopped parsley	1 tablespoon freshly chopped parsley
salt and freshly ground black pepper	salt and freshly ground black pepper
8 oz (225 g) peeled prawns, well drained	1⅓ cups shelled shrimp, well drained
a few sprigs fresh dill	a few sprigs fresh dill
6 oz (175 g) red cabbage, finely shredded	6 oz red cabbage, finely shredded
3 spring onions, chopped	3 scallions, chopped
½ teaspoon dried dill weed	½ teaspoon dried dill weed
2 large carrots	2 large carrots
juice of ½ lemon	juice of ½ lemon
1 bunch watercress, stalks and tatty leaves removed	1 bunch watercress, cleaned

Put one egg on the side of each plate, coat with a little mayonnaise and garnish with a rolled up anchovy fillet.

Put half the French dressing in the bottom of a bowl, add the shredded lettuce, parsley and seasoning and mix well. Put a portion of this salad next to the egg. Next put a portion of prawns, working round the plate, and decorate with a sprig of fresh dill.

In another bowl mix the red cabbage, spring onions (scallions) and dried dill. Season and mix well with the remaining French dressing, then put a portion of this next to the prawns.

Grate the carrot and toss in the lemon juice and put a portion of this next to the red cabbage and finally fill the gap between the egg and red cabbage with sprigs of watercress. Serve immediately.

Serves 6

Gingered Grapefruit

Light, appetising and refreshing, grapefruit supply fibre and Vitamin C – an ideal way to start a meal.

Imperial/metric	American
2 large grapefruit, halved	2 large grapefruit, halved
2 oz (50 g) stem ginger	⅓ cup preserved ginger
2 tablespoons runny honey	2 tablespoons liquid honey
a little dark muscovado sugar	a little dark brown sugar

Separate the grapefruit segments with a sharp knife. Slice the stem ginger (preserved ginger) and arrange around the outside of each of the grapefruit. Spoon a little honey onto the centre of each half and sprinkle with a little muscovado sugar.

Grill (broil) under a hot grill (broiler) for about 5 minutes until the sugar has melted, and the grapefruit is warmed through.

Serves 4

Hazelnut (Filbert) Roulade

This makes rather a different first course and is also ideal for a vegetarian. If you're watching your weight, you could use a low-fat cream cheese like Quark. Serve with a good tasty, preferably home-made, chutney.

Imperial/metric	American
2 eggs	2 eggs
1½ oz (40 g) light muscovado sugar	3 tablespoons light brown sugar
1 oz (25 g) self-raising flour	¼ cup self-rising flour
1 oz (25 g) plain wholewheat flour	¼ cup wholewheat flour
1 oz (25 g) hazelnuts, finely chopped	¼ cup filberts, finely chopped

Filling	Filling
8 oz (225 g) cream cheese	1 cup cream cheese
1 tablespoon freshly chopped chives	1 tablespoon freshly chopped chives
1 fat clove of garlic, crushed	1 whole clove of garlic, crushed
freshly ground black pepper	freshly ground black pepper
skimmed milk	skim milk

Heat the oven to 425°F/220°C/Gas 7. Lightly grease and line a 7×11 inch (17.5×27.5 cm) Swiss roll tin (jelly roll pan) with greased greaseproof paper (non-stick parchment).

Put the eggs and sugar in a bowl and beat with an electric whisk for several minutes until the mixture leaves a trail when the whisk is lifted out. Gently fold in the flours and nuts until evenly blended. Turn into the prepared tin (jelly roll pan), level out, then bake in the oven for about 8 minutes until golden brown. Turn out on to a clean sheet of greaseproof paper (non-stick parchment), remove the paper (parchment) the roulade was cooked in, and roll the roulade up like a Swiss roll (jelly roll) with a fresh sheet of greaseproof paper (non-stick parchment) inside and around to prevent it sticking. Allow to cool.

For the filling, put the cream cheese in a bowl, mash down with a fork then blend in the chives, garlic, pepper and enough skimmed milk to give a spreading consistency.

Once the roulade has cooled, unroll, remove the paper (parchment), and spread the cream cheese filling over the roulade. Re-roll, and chill well before serving. To serve, divide into eight slices and arrange two on each serving plate garnished with a little salad.

Serves 4

Nutcracker Salad

This is an ideal first course to serve if you are entertaining a vegetarian friend. It's also very good for *you*!

Imperial/metric	American
6 oz (175 g) beansprouts	3 cups beansprouts
2 oz (50 g) sunflower seeds	⅓ cup sunflower seeds
½ cucumber	½ cucumber
2 oz (50 g) stoned raisins	⅓ cup raisins, chopped
2 oz (50 g) salted cashew nuts	⅓ cup salted cashew nuts
4 radishes, sliced	4 red radishes, sliced
salt and freshly ground black pepper	salt and freshly ground black pepper
¼ pint (150 ml) low calorie dressing (see page 135)	⅔ cup low calorie dressing (see page 135)
1 tablespoon freshly chopped mint	1 tablespoon freshly chopped mint

Put the beansprouts and sunflower seeds in a bowl. Cut the cucumber in half lengthways, scoop out and discard the seeds, then slice the cucumber to give moon-shaped pieces of cucumber. Add these to the beansprouts with the remaining ingredients. Mix well, and taste to check seasoning.

Divide salad between four serving plates and garnish with sprigs of fresh mint.

Serves 4

Asparagus in French Dressing

English asparagus is available only in May, June and part of July. (However, as a stand-by, I usually have cans of asparagus in the store cupboard so I can always fall back on this starter in an emergency.) Fresh asparagus is an unadulterated, delicious vegetable, and it's packed with Vitamins A, B and C, and contains very few calories (not true, sadly, of traditional accompaniments like melted butter).

Imperial/metric	American
1 lb (450 g) asparagus	*1 lb asparagus*
salt	*salt*
¼ pint (150 ml) French dressing (see page 134)	*⅔ cup French dressing (see page 134)*
freshly chopped parsley	*freshly chopped parsley*

Cut off the woody ends of the asparagus, tie in three bundles and lay them in a shallow pan. Add about a teaspoon of salt, cover with boiling water and then bring back to the boil and simmer for about 10 minutes or until tender. Drain well, remove the string, arrange in a serving dish and allow to cool.

Pour over the French dressing then chill well in the refrigerator. Just before serving sprinkle with a little freshly chopped parsley.

Serves 4

Stuffed Tomatoes

Mushroom stalks can often be bought very cheaply from the green-grocer and are perfect for this recipe. It could also be a light and healthy lunch served with a green salad.

Imperial/metric	American
6 large beefsteak tomatoes	6 large beefsteak tomatoes
2 oz (50 g) ham, chopped	¾ cup chopped smoked ham
2 oz (50 g) mushrooms (or stalks), chopped	½ cup chopped mushrooms
2 oz (50 g) fresh brown breadcrumbs	1 cup fresh soft brown breadcrumbs
1 tablespoon freshly chopped parsley	1 tablespoon freshly chopped parsley
salt and freshly ground black pepper	salt and freshly ground black pepper
1 egg, beaten	1 egg, beaten
3 oz (75 g) mature Cheddar cheese, grated	¾ cup grated aged Cheddar cheese
a little sunflower oil	a little sunflower oil

Heat the oven to 350°F/180°C/Gas 4, and lightly grease an ovenproof dish.

Cut a small slice from the top of each tomato and carefully scoop out the pulp from inside. (Discard half of this pulp as it is too much to put back in the tomatoes: add to a soup or stew.)

Add the ham, mushrooms, breadcrumbs, parsley, seasoning and egg to the remaining tomato pulp and mix well. Spoon this filling into the tomato cases, top with cheese and replace the lids.

Arrange in the ovenproof dish so that they are just touching, brush with a little oil and cook in the oven for about 20 minutes until the cheese has melted and is bubbling.

Serves 6

Good Onion Soup

Everyone knows that onions are healthy, and this soup will warm on a cold day.

Fry the onions gently so that they become a golden brown without catching at the edges, which ensures a soup with a very good flavour.

Imperial/metric	American
1 oz (25 g) butter	2 tablespoons butter
1 tablespoon sunflower oil	1 tablespoon sunflower oil
1 lb (450 g) onions, finely chopped	4 cups chopped onion
1 oz (25 g) flour	¼ cup all-purpose flour
1½ pints (900 ml) good beef stock	3¾ cups good beef stock
salt and freshly ground black pepper	salt and freshly ground black pepper
dash of gravy browning	dash gravy coloring
2 oz (50 g) well flavoured Cheddar cheese, grated	½ cup grated aged Cheddar cheese

Heat the butter and oil in a saucepan, and gently fry onions until golden brown (this will take a while but be patient). Stir in the flour and cook for a minute then gradually blend in the stock. Bring to the boil, stirring until slightly thickened. Season with salt and pepper and add just a dash of gravy browning to give a good colour.

Cover the pan with a lid and simmer gently for about 45 minutes until the onion is tender. Taste and check seasoning, then serve piping hot sprinkled with cheese.

Serves 4

Minestrone Soup

Quick and easy to prepare, this soup contains a lot of healthy vegetables, so makes a filling start to a meal. The recipe makes a large
quantity, so some can be frozen for another day.

Imperial/metric	American
8 oz (225 g) broad beans	2 cups lima beans
3 sticks celery, chopped	3 stalks celery, chopped
1 onion, sliced	1 onion, sliced
2 cloves of garlic, crushed	2 whole cloves of garlic, crushed
8 oz (225 g) tomatoes, skinned and quartered	2 cups tomatoes, skinned and quartered
8 oz (225 g) spinach, finely chopped	2 cups finely chopped raw spinach
2 carrots, diced	2 carrots, diced
4 oz (100 g) brown rice	$\frac{1}{2}$ cup brown rice
2 tablespoons freshly chopped parsley	2 tablespoons freshly chopped parsley
3 pints (1.75 litres) good beef stock	7$\frac{1}{2}$ cups good beef stock
salt and freshly ground black pepper	salt and freshly ground black pepper
Parmesan cheese	Parmesan cheese

Measure all the ingredients (except the cheese) into the largest saucepan you have. Bring to the boil, then reduce the heat, cover the pan with
a lid and simmer gently for about an hour until all the vegetables are
tender.

Taste and check seasoning, then pour into serving bowls and sprinkle
with a little Parmesan cheese.

Serves about 8

Lentil Soup

Like most pulses, lentils are very high in food value. If you have none in the store cupboard, split peas will act as a good substitute in this recipe.

Imperial/metric	American
8 oz (225 g) orange lentils	1 cup lentils
1 large onion, chopped	1 large onion, chopped
3 sticks celery, chopped	3 stalks celery, chopped
2 medium potatoes, diced	2 medium sized potatoes, diced
2 pints (1.2 litres) good chicken stock	5 cups good chicken stock
salt and freshly ground black pepper	salt and freshly ground black pepper

Put the lentils in a bowl, cover with cold water and leave overnight.

Drain lentils and discard water. Put all the ingredients in a large saucepan. Bring to the boil then cover the saucepan with a lid, reduce heat and simmer for about an hour until the lentils are tender.

Allow soup to cool slightly then reduce to a purée in a processor or blender. Rinse out the saucepan, return soup and reheat before serving. Serve very hot.

Serves 6

Hearty Soup

This soup is a meal in itself, offering both meat protein and vegetable goodness. Serve on a cold winter's day as a starter, or it would make a nourishing mugful for those just home from school or work.

Imperial/metric

1 lb (450 g) lean stewing steak
2 tablespoons sunflower oil
1 lb (450 g) onions, chopped
1 tablespoon paprika pepper
14 oz (397 g) can peeled
   tomatoes
1½ pints (900 ml) good beef
   stock
1 lb (450 g) potatoes, diced
2 medium carrots, chopped
1 small green pepper, chopped
salt and freshly ground black
   pepper

American

1 lb lean stewing steak
2 tablespoons sunflower oil
4 cups chopped onion
1 tablespoon paprika pepper
1½ cups canned tomatoes
3¾ cups good beef stock
2⅔ cups diced raw potato
2 medium carrots, chopped
1 small green pepper, chopped
salt and freshly ground black
   pepper

Cut the meat into very small cubes. Heat the oil in a saucepan and fry meat and onion for about 10 minutes until browned all over. Stir in paprika, tomatoes and stock, then bring to the boil, stirring continuously.

Cover saucepan with a lid, reduce the heat and simmer for about an hour. Then add the potato, carrots and green pepper, and cook for about a further 30 minutes until the meat and vegetables are tender.

Taste and check seasoning then serve piping hot.

Serves 6

Cream of Tomato Soup

Tomato soup is always a favourite with children, and this recipe is particularly quick and easy to prepare – as well as being low in calories!

Imperial/metric	American
knob of polyunsaturated margarine	1 tablespoon margarine
1 tablespoon sunflower oil	1 tablespoon sunflower oil
1 large onion, finely chopped	1 large onion, finely chopped
2 oz (50 g) flour	½ cup all-purpose flour
1 pint (600 ml) water	2½ cups water
1 pint (600 ml) skimmed milk	2½ cups skim milk
5 oz (150 g) can tomato purée	½ cup tomato purée
2 teaspoons light muscovado sugar	2 teaspoons light brown sugar
salt and freshly ground black pepper	salt and freshly ground black pepper
freshly chopped parsley	freshly chopped parsley

Heat the margarine and oil in a saucepan, add onion, and fry gently for about 10 minutes until pale golden brown. Stir in the flour and cook for a minute. Blend in the water and then the milk, and bring to the boil, stirring until slightly thickened. Add the purée, sugar and seasoning, and simmer gently for about 20 minutes until the onion is tender.

Taste and check seasoning, then serve hot sprinkled with a little freshly chopped parsley.

Serves 4

Chestnut Soup

Dried chestnuts are available in most health-food shops and deli-catessens.

They make a filling and tasty soup.

Imperial/metric

6 oz (175 g) dried chestnuts
1 tablespoon sunflower oil
knob of polyunsaturated
   margarine
1 large onion, chopped
2 pints (1.2 litres) good chicken
   stock
salt and freshly ground black
   pepper
3 tablespoons inexpensive sherry

American

1½ cups dried chestnuts
1 tablespoon sunflower oil
1 tablespoon margarine
1 large onion, chopped
5 cups good chicken stock
salt and freshly ground black
   pepper
3 tablespoons inexpensive sherry

Put the chestnuts in a bowl, cover with cold water and leave to soak overnight. Drain well.

Heat the oil and margarine in a saucepan and fry onion and chestnuts for about 5 minutes until the onion is pale golden brown. Stir in the stock and seasoning. Cover with a lid and simmer gently for about 45 minutes then reduce to a purée in a processor or blender (with this quantity of soup, it may be necessary to do it in batches).

Return to the saucepan, stir in sherry and bring back to the boil. Taste and check seasoning then serve hot in bowls.

Serves 4

Chilled Cucumber Soup

This is a wonderfully refreshing soup for a hot day. It is also wonderfully slimming, as cucumbers consist of almost 96 per cent water!

Imperial/metric	American
1 cucumber, sliced	1 cucumber, sliced
15 oz (425 g) can consommé	2 cups canned consommé
a small bunch of watercress	a small bunch of watercress
salt and freshly ground black pepper	salt and freshly ground black pepper
¼ pint (150 ml) natural yogurt	⅔ cup unflavored yogurt

Put the cucumber and consommé in a saucepan and bring to the boil. Trim the thicker stalks off the watercress and add the leaves to the saucepan with some seasoning. Cover with a lid and simmer gently for about 15 minutes until the watercress is tender.

Turn the soup into a processor or blender and reduce to a purée with the yogurt. Pour into a bowl, cover with clingfilm (plastic wrap) and chill in the refrigerator for several hours. Taste and check seasoning before serving.

Serves 4

Farmhouse Pâté

Meat or fish starters are more substantial than many vegetable first courses or soups, but can be served when the main course is lighter, or as a starter on a special occasion. The livers contain iron, Vitamins A and B.

Imperial/metric	American
1 bay leaf	*1 bay leaf*
6 rashers streaky bacon, derinded	*6 bacon slices*
1 egg	*1 egg*
4 oz (100 g) fresh brown breadcrumbs	*2 cups fresh soft brown breadcrumbs*
4 tablespoons port	*4 tablespoons port*
8 oz (225 g) chicken livers	*8 oz chicken liver*
8 oz (225 g) pig's liver	*8 oz pork liver*
4 oz (100 g) bacon trimmings	*½ cup chopped bacon*
1 fat clove of garlic, crushed	*1 whole clove of garlic, crushed*
salt and freshly ground black pepper	*salt and freshly ground black pepper*
½ teaspoon ground nutmeg	*½ teaspoon ground nutmeg*
¼ teaspoon dried mixed herbs	*¼ teaspoon dried mixed herbs*
½ level teaspoon dried marjoram	*½ level teaspoon dried marjoram*
4 oz (100 g) lard, melted	*½ cup shortening, melted*

Grease a 2 pint/1.2 litre (5 cup) ovenproof terrine and put the bay leaf in the bottom. Stretch the slices of bacon with the back of a knife on a board, and use to line the sides and base of the terrine.

Put all the other ingredients in a processor or blender and reduce to a purée (if using a blender it may be necessary to do this in two batches).

Pour pâté into prepared dish, and cover with a lid or piece of foil. Put dish in a roasting tin containing ½ inch (1 cm) warm water and bake in the oven at 325°F/160°C/Gas 3 for about 2½ hours, when the pâté will have shrunk slightly from the sides of the dish. Remove lid or foil, then cover with a clean piece of foil, and weigh down with several weights.

Refrigerate overnight before turning out.

Serves 8

Smoked Mackerel Pâté

This is a delicious light fish pâté to serve as a first course. For a change try making it with smoked salmon pieces or smoked trout instead of mackerel.

Imperial/metric	American
12 oz (350 g) smoked mackerel (approximately 2 large fillets)	*2 large fillets smoked mackerel*
8 oz (225 g) curd cheese	*1 cup curd cheese*
3 oz (75 g) polyunsaturated margarine	*⅓ cup margarine*
juice of ¼ lemon	*juice of ¼ lemon*
a little grated nutmeg	*a little grated nutmeg*
freshly ground black pepper	*freshly ground black pepper*
chopped parsley	*chopped parsley*

Remove the skin from the mackerel fillets, roughly break up the flesh and put in a processor or blender with the remaining ingredients (excluding the parsley). Process for a few moments until thoroughly blended. Taste and check seasoning.

Turn into a 1 pint/600 ml (2½ cup) pâté or terrine dish, sprinkle with parsley, and chill in the refrigerator until set. Serve with hot wholewheat toast and a little salad.

Serves 6–8

Mini Muffin Pizzas

Children in particular adore these mini pizzas, which make a quick and healthy snack. Wholewheat muffins are available in most supermarkets and are a lovely light base for a pizza. You could use the granary rolls on page 170 if you like.

Imperial/metric

1 oz (25 g) polyunsaturated margarine
8 oz (225 g) onion, chopped
14 oz (397 g) can tomatoes
½ teaspoon mixed dried herbs
salt and freshly ground black pepper
6 wholemeal muffins
6 oz (175 g) mature Cheddar cheese, grated
2 oz (50 g) anchovy fillets, drained

American

2 tablespoons margarine
2 cups chopped onion
1½ cups canned tomatoes
½ teaspoon dried mixed herbs
salt and freshly ground black pepper
6 wholewheat muffins
1½ cups grated aged Cheddar cheese
¼ cup anchovy fillets, drained

Melt the margarine in a saucepan and quickly fry onion for about 5 minutes until beginning to soften, then add the contents of the can of tomatoes. Continue to cook for a further 5 minutes or until the mixture has reduced to a thick pulp. Add the herbs and season to taste.

Slice the muffins in half horizontally and divide the tomato mixture between them, spreading it out evenly over the tops of the muffins. Sprinkle with cheese and arrange the anchovy fillets on top.

Heat the grill (broiler), lift pizzas on to grill (broiler) pan and grill (broil) for about 8 minutes until the cheese has melted and is bubbling.

Makes 12 mini pizzas

Party Granary Rolls (Wholewheat Buns)

These are of course nicest if you make your own rolls – for which, see page 170 – but you can always buy them from good bakers (wholewheat rolls are good too).

Imperial/metric	American
6 granary bread rolls (page 170)	6 wholewheat breadbuns (page 170)
6 rashers bacon, derinded	6 Canadian bacon slices
3 hard-boiled eggs	3 hard-cooked eggs
2 tablespoons mayonnaise (see page 132)	2 tablespoons mayonnaise (see page 132)
salt and freshly ground black pepper	salt and freshly ground black pepper
3 tomatoes, sliced	3 tomatoes, sliced
4 oz (100 g) cream cheese (low-fat if you like)	½ cup cream cheese (low-fat if you like)
a small bunch watercress, stems trimmed and tatty leaves removed	a small bunch watercress, cleaned

Make four cuts in each bread roll (breadbun), one horizontally across the bottom, and three vertical slits in the top large enough to take the filling.

Grill (broil) the bacon under a hot grill (broiler) until crispy and use to fill the bottom slit in the rolls (buns). Roughly chop the eggs and mix with the mayonnaise and seasoning, then use to fill one of the outside slits on top of the rolls (buns). Slice the tomatoes and use to fill the other outside slit on top of the rolls (buns). Spread the middle slit with cream cheese and arrange the watercress in this slit right on top of the rolls (buns) so that it is poking out of the sides.

Serves 6

Special Sandwich Fillings

Sandwiches are one of my favourite lunches, they need not be boring if you choose moist fillings and are generous with them. Always use fresh good wholemeal bread, and because the fillings are moist, you need not use butter.

EGG AND CHIVE

Imperial/metric

3 hard-boiled eggs
2 tablespoons mayonnaise (see page 132)
2 teaspoons freshly chopped chives
salt and freshly ground black pepper

American

3 hard-cooked eggs
2 tablespoons mayonnaise (see page 132)
2 teaspoons freshly chopped chives
salt and freshly ground black pepper

Roughly chop the eggs then bind together with the mayonnaise and chives. Season to taste.

CREAM CHEESE AND CELERY

Imperial/metric

8 oz (225 g) cream cheese (low-fat if you like)
a little skimmed milk
4 sticks celery, chopped
salt and freshly ground black pepper

American

1 cup cream cheese (low-fat if you like)
a little skim milk
4 stalks celery, chopped
salt and freshly ground black pepper

Beat the cream cheese with the milk to give a spreading consistency then stir in the celery and seasoning.

PRAWN (SHELLED SHRIMP) AND LETTUCE

Imperial/metric	American
8 oz (225 g) peeled prawns	1½ cups shelled shrimp
2 tablespoons garlic mayonnaise (see page 132)	2 tablespoons garlic mayonnaise (see page 132)
salt and freshly ground black pepper	salt and freshly ground black pepper
shredded lettuce	shredded lettuce

Drain the prawns (shelled shrimp) well on kitchen paper towels then mix with the mayonnaise and seasoning. Fill sandwich with prawn (shrimp) mixture and shredded lettuce.

Pitta Bread Brunch

This way of serving pitta bread will satisfy the hungriest of appetites. Add some salad ingredients – lettuce, sliced tomato or cucumber – for extra taste and goodness.

Imperial/metric	American
2 wholemeal pitta breads	2 wholewheat pitta breads
4 eggs	4 eggs
2 tablespoons water	2 tablespoons water
salt and freshly ground black pepper	salt and freshly ground black pepper
1 oz (25 g) butter	2 tablespoons butter

Make a slit along the sides of the pitta bread and open out ready for the filling.

Put the eggs, water and seasoning in a bowl and beat lightly with a fork. Heat an omelette pan until hot, add half the butter and when hot and frothy pour in half the egg mixture. Using a fork, quickly draw mixture from the sides of the pan to the centre to allow the uncooked egg to run underneath, shake the pan and leave for a few seconds. Draw the pan from the heat, loosen the sides, fold the omelette in half and slip inside one of the pitta breads.

Repeat with the remaining egg mixture and eat hot as a sandwich.

Serves 2

GOOD FAMILY MAIN MEALS

Fish is a very good choice for the family as it is rich in vitamins (especially the rare D, of which oily fish are a major source), is lower in fat than meat, and adds variety to the week's meals. Sadly, over the past five years I have seen no less than four wet fish shops close in our area – and this is going on over much of the country. However new supermarkets have opened with good fish sections, and I notice that the trend now seems to be to extend these. When buying fish, I very often arrive at the counter not having made up my mind, then I buy what looks best at a reasonable cost. Fish have expensive and cheap seasons just like vegetables! We also shop at trout farms. Farming trout has brought the price down so these luxury fish are now available for family meals – and going to a farm makes a fun outing for the children.

Meat of all sorts is good for family meals, but I now take great care to avoid fat. When planning meals and when choosing meat, I go for non-fatty cuts and meats whenever I can. Chicken and turkey are best: there is little fat, but you should avoid eating the skin. Chickens are often good 'special offers' to freeze away; and do look out for casserole turkey meat which is often very reasonable, and can be used for any of the casserole recipes I include. Game birds, too, contain less fat than red meat.

Lamb and venison are slightly less fatty than beef or pork, and you must never forget that the flesh itself – of any meat – contains a lot of hidden fat. Always try to cook by the least fatty methods, *using* less fat, and skimming *off* fat before serving. (A good way of doing this with casserole-type dishes is to refrigerate them overnight and then just lift off the fat layer the next day.)

Of course, minced (ground) meat plays an important part in meal planning for most budget-conscious families, and though it may be high in fat, you can minimise the problem by knowledgeable shopping and cooking. Look for bright red minced beef with only a low proportion of the yellow which indicates fat. Better still, if you have a processor, buy, say, 4 lb (1.8 kg) of a cut from the forequarter of beef, and mince it yourself. Use some and freeze the rest, labelling it so you remember to use it within 4–6 weeks. You can also buy the beef and ask the butcher to mince (grind) it for you – ask for this to be done on a quiet day, not a busy Saturday morning! And when cooking the minced (ground) meat, dry-fry it gently in a non-stick frying pan until the fat runs out of the meat, and then fry as usual. Skim as much fat away as you can.

And, incidentally, when making main meals from cheese, do bear in mind that though it is an excellent food – high in protein and containing valuable vitamins – it is also high in fat. If you can restrict the amount of cheese eaten by each member of the family to a piece the size of an ordinary matchbox each day, do (it helps to *grate* cheese so that it *looks* like a big generous mound!). Eggs, too, are good for main meals, but try to restrict their use throughout the week.

When serving main meals, do not automatically put out a salt cellar. Tell the family that you have checked the seasoning yourself and that no more should be needed. Encourage them to cut back gradually, if necessary, and use less in cooking over all. Salt is a compound of sodium, and it is now believed that we should avoid giving too much of it to the family. Sodium is present in bacon, shellfish, ham and processed foods of various sorts – so be wary when planning to include these in the family's meals for the week. Cut back in every way as much as you can.

Cod Provençal

White fish like cod, sole and plaice, are good slimmer's food, containing little fat, but plenty of the proteins, vitamins and minerals necessary in a good healthy diet.

Prawns (shrimp) can be used instead of the scampi (jumbo shrimp) if preferred.

Imperial/metric

1 oz (25 g) polyunsaturated margarine
1 medium onion, chopped
4 oz (100 g) button mushrooms, sliced
14 oz (397 g) can tomatoes
1 teaspoon light muscovado sugar
salt and freshly ground black pepper
2 tablespoons freshly chopped parsley
6 oz (175 g) peeled scampi tails
1 lb (450 g) fillet of cod, divided into 4 equal pieces

American

1 tablespoon margarine
1 medium onion, chopped
1 cup sliced mushrooms
1½ cups canned tomatoes
1 teaspoon light brown sugar
salt and freshly ground black pepper
2 tablespoons freshly chopped parsley
1½ cups jumbo shrimp
1 lb cod fillets, divided into 4 equal pieces

Melt the margarine in a saucepan and quickly fry onion for about 5 minutes until soft. Add mushrooms and the contents of the can of tomatoes, bring to the boil, and simmer until thick and pulpy. Stir in sugar, seasoning to taste, half the parsley, and the scampi (jumbo shrimp). Turn into a 2 pint/1.2 litre (5 cup) ovenproof dish.

Arrange the pieces of cod on top of the sauce then bake in the oven at 375°F/180°C/Gas 5 for about 25 minutes until the fish is cooked.

Serve sprinkled with remaining chopped parsley, and accompanied by a crisp green vegetable such as peas, beans or broccoli.

Serves 4

Hedgerley Cod

This is a complete main meal in one dish, no need for separate vegetables.

Imperial/metric	American
6 oz (175 g) brown rice	¾ cup brown rice
4 cod cutlets	4 cod steaks
1 oz (25 g) polyunsaturated margarine	1 tablespoon margarine
1 oz (25 g) flour	¼ cup all-purpose flour
½ pint (300 ml) skimmed milk	1¼ cups skim milk
freshly ground black pepper	freshly ground black pepper
8 oz (225 g) tomatoes	4 tomatoes
4 oz (100 g) mature Cheddar cheese, grated	1 cup grated aged Cheddar cheese

Cook the rice in plenty of boiling salted water as directed on the packet. Rinse and drain thoroughly.

Lightly grease a large shallow ovenproof dish and arrange the rice around the outside of the dish. Put the cod cutlets in the centre. Heat the margarine in a small saucepan, add the flour and cook for a minute. Gradually blend in the milk, bring to the boil, stirring until thickened. Season well with pepper and pour sauce over the fish.

Slice the tomatoes thickly and arrange on top of rice around the edge of the dish. Sprinkle the cheese all over. Cook in the oven at 400°F/200°C/ Gas 6 for about 30 minutes until the cheese is golden brown and the fish is tender.

Serves 4

Stuffed Lemon Sole

Use any flat fish that looks a good buy when you are at the fishmongers.

Imperial/metric	American
2 oz (50 g) fresh brown breadcrumbs	1 cup soft fresh brown breadcrumbs
2 tablespoons freshly chopped parsley	2 tablespoons freshly chopped parsley
a little fresh thyme	a little fresh thyme
3 spring onions, finely chopped	3 scallions, finely chopped
grated rind and juice of 1 lemon	grated rind and juice of 1 lemon
salt and freshly ground black pepper	salt and freshly ground black pepper
1 egg	1 egg
2 (12 oz/350 g) whole lemon sole	2 whole lemon sole
a little butter	a little butter
1 tomato	1 tomato

Put the breadcrumbs in a bowl with the parsley, thyme, onions (scallions), lemon rind and juice and seasoning. Lightly beat the egg and stir into the breadcrumbs, mixing all well together.

Clean and remove the head from the fish, and trim fins and tail with scissors. Place each fish, dark-skinned side down, on a board and with a sharp knife make a cut through the white skin along the backbone to within ¾ inch (1.5 cm) of the head and tail. Ease the flesh away from either side of the bone to form two large pockets. Fill with stuffing.

Lightly butter a shallow ovenproof dish, and lay the fish on it. Dot with a little more butter, cover with a piece of foil and cook in the oven at 350°F/180°C/Gas 4 for about 30 minutes until the fish is just tender. Slice the tomato, arrange on top of stuffing and return to the oven for a further 10 minutes.

To serve lift the fish onto warmed serving plates and serve with a fresh green vegetable.

Serves 2

Cornish Parcel Pie

This pie can be served either warm or cold, accompanied by a crisp green salad.

Imperial/metric

6 oz (175 g) strong plain flour
2 oz (50 g) wholemeal flour
1 teaspoon baking powder
6 oz (175 g) block margarine,
 well chilled
about ¼ pint (150 ml) cold water
a little beaten egg to glaze

American

1½ cups bread flour
½ cup wholewheat flour
1 teaspoon baking powder
¾ cup hard margarine, well
 chilled
about ⅔ cup cold water
a little beaten egg to glaze

Filling

1 lb (450 g) boneless cod
4 oz (100 g) brown rice, cooked
3 oz (75 g) peeled prawns
2 tablespoons freshly chopped
 parsley
juice of ½ lemon
salt and freshly ground black
 pepper
5 oz (142 g) carton natural
 yogurt (or home-made, see
 page 17)
a little beaten egg to glaze

Filling

1 lb boneless cod fillets
½ cup brown rice, cooked
½ cup shelled shrimp
2 tablespoons freshly chopped
 parsley
juice of ½ lemon
salt and freshly ground black
 pepper
⅔ cup unflavored yogurt
a little beaten egg to glaze

Start by preparing the pastry. Measure the flours and baking powder into a bowl and grate the margarine into the middle with a coarse grater (flour grater and hands if the margarine starts to become sticky). Mix to a soft dough with the water.

Turn out onto a lightly floured surface, knead gently to give a smooth dough, then roll out to an oblong. Fold in three as if you were making flaky pastry, wrap in clingfilm (plastic wrap) and chill for about 15 minutes. Roll out pastry and repeat this process three more times. Chill in the refrigerator until required.

For the filling, poach the cod in a little water until cooked (the flesh will flake easily). Remove from the heat and allow to cool, then transfer to a mixing bowl and roughly flake flesh. Stir in the rice, prawns, parsley, lemon juice, seasoning and yogurt and mix until thoroughly blended.

Heat the oven to 425°F/220°C/Gas 7. Roll out pastry to an 11 inch (27.5 cm) square and lift on to a baking tray (cookie tray). Spoon filling into the middle, dampen edges of pastry with water and fold up, to seal in the filling, like an envelope. If necessary, trim edges of pastry to straighten the sides and use trimmings to make pastry leaves for decoration. Brush with beaten egg and bake in the oven for about 35 minutes until golden brown.

Serve hot with Real Tomato Sauce (see page 130)

Serves 4

Plaice Florentine

This dish, too, is a meal in itself. Plaice is filling and healthy, and the spinach and cheese add extra goodness and flavour.

Imperial/metric

4 large fillets of plaice, skinned
salt and freshly ground black
   pepper
juice of ½ lemon
2 oz (50 g) polyunsaturated
   margarine
2 oz (50 g) flour
1 pint (600 ml) skimmed milk
1½ lb (675 g) fresh spinach,
   cooked and well drained
2 oz (50 g) well flavoured
   Cheddar cheese, grated
1 oz (25 g) fresh brown
   breadcrumbs

American

4 large fillets of plaice, skinned
salt and freshly ground black
   pepper
juice of ½ lemon
¼ cup margarine
½ cup flour
2½ cups skim milk
1½ lb fresh spinach, cooked and
   well drained
½ cup grated aged Cheddar
   cheese
½ cup soft fresh brown
   breadcrumbs

Heat the oven to 400°F/200°C/Gas 6. Season the fillets and sprinkle with lemon juice, then roll up.

Melt the margarine in a saucepan, add the flour and cook for a minute. Gradually blend in the milk and bring to the boil, stirring until thickened. Season to taste. Blend about ¼ pint/150 ml (⅔ cup) of the sauce with the spinach and put in a 2 pint/1.2 litre (5 cup) ovenproof dish. Arrange the fillets of fish on top and spoon the remaining sauce over them. Mix the cheese and breadcrumbs together and sprinkle over the dish.

Cook uncovered in the oven for about 20 minutes until the top is golden brown and the fish perfectly white.

Serves 4

Trout with Cashew Nuts

Cashew nuts have a delicious flavour, and they are often quite reasonable if bought broken or as pieces. They are a good food, like other nuts, containing considerable vitamin and mineral value.

Imperial/metric	American
4 trout, cleaned	*4 trout, cleaned*
seasoned wholewheat flour	*seasoned wholewheat flour*
1 oz (25 g) butter	*⅛ cup butter*
2 tablespoons sunflower oil	*2 tablespoons sunflower oil*
2 oz (50 g) unsalted broken cashew nuts	*½ cup unsalted broken cashew nuts*
lemon wedges and fresh parsley to garnish	*lemon wedges and parsley to garnish*

Wash the trout under running cold water to remove any loose blood. (If the trout have not been cleaned, slit them along the belly with a sharp knife and remove the gut; wash thoroughly and remove the eyes.)

Coat the trout in seasoned flour. Melt the butter and most of the oil in a large frying pan (skillet) and fry the fish for about 8 minutes, turning once. Remove from the pan (skillet) and arrange on a warm serving dish.

Add the remaining oil to the pan with the cashew nuts and fry quickly until golden brown. Pour the cashew nut and butter sauce over the trout and garnish with lemon wedges and parsley.

Serves 4

Rice Seafood Sensation

A sort of wonderful kedgeree, delicious for lunch, or as a first course for 8–10 people. It's also rather healthy, as seafood in general is rich in many vitamins and minerals, particularly the trace element, iodine.

Imperial/metric

8 oz (225 g) brown rice
1 lb (450 g) smoked haddock, poached
4 oz (100 g) fresh cooked mussels
4 oz (100 g) fresh cooked cockles
8 oz (225 g) fresh cooked, shelled prawns
4 crab sticks, cut in four
4 hard-boiled eggs, roughly chopped
2 tablespoons freshly chopped parsley
juice of ½ lemon
salt and freshly ground black pepper
6 cooked jumbo prawns in the shell, to garnish

American

1 cup brown rice
1 lb smoked haddock (poached)
¾ cup fresh cooked mussels
¾ cup fresh cooked cockles
1½ cups shelled shrimp
4 crab sticks, cut in four
4 hard-cooked eggs, roughly chopped
2 tablespoons freshly chopped parsley
juice of ½ lemon
salt and freshly ground black pepper
6 shrimp in the shell, to garnish

Cook the rice in boiling salted water as directed on the packet. Drain well and allow to cool. Flake the smoked fish and add to the rice with the remaining ingredients. Mix well then turn into a serving dish and garnish with the large prawns.

Serve with a fresh green salad and garlic mayonnaise (see page 132).

Serves 6

Somerset Mackerel

Mackerel, although an oily fish, is particularly rich in Vitamin B_6 and Vitamin D. Serve straight from the oven garnished with lemon wedges and a little fresh parsley, accompanied by crisp, green broccoli and baked tomatoes, perhaps.

Imperial/metric	American
4 fresh mackerel, cleaned, heads and guts removed	4 fresh mackerel, cleaned
salt and freshly ground black pepper	salt and freshly ground black pepper
2 Cox's apples	2 dessert apples
1 small onion	1 small onion
2 oz (50 g) fresh brown breadcrumbs	1 cup fresh soft brown breadcrumbs
6 oz (175 g) mature Cheddar cheese, grated	1½ cups grated aged Cheddar cheese
¼ pint (150 ml) dry cider	⅔ cup hard cider
lemon wedges and fresh parsley to garnish	lemon wedges and parsley to garnish

Heat the oven to 350°F/180°C/Gas 4. Rinse the fish well under running cold water and dry thoroughly with kitchen paper towels. Season with salt and pepper.

Peel and coarsely grate the apples and the onion. Mix in a bowl with the breadcrumbs and half the cheese. Stuff the mackerel with this mixture and secure the opening of each fish with two or three wooden cocktail sticks (toothpicks).

Arrange the fish side by side in a shallow ovenproof dish so that they are just touching. Sprinkle with the remaining cheese and pour over the cider.

Cover with foil and bake in the oven for about 30 minutes until cooked through and a golden brown. (The flesh of the fish will flake easily once cooked.) Garnish with lemon wedges and fresh parsley.

Serves 4

Stuffed Herrings in Foil

Herrings are usually a good reasonable buy. Cooking them this way avoids any fishy smells, as well as ensuring that all the goodness of the fish is retained in the individual packages.

Imperial/metric	American
3 herrings	3 herrings
3 teaspoons Dijon mustard	3 teaspoons Dijon mustard
salt and freshly ground black pepper	salt and freshly ground black pepper
butter	butter
lemon slices and fresh parsley to garnish	lemon slices and fresh parsley to garnish

Cut the heads off the herrings using a sharp knife. Cut along the underside of each fish from head to tail and remove any roe and gut. Wash under running cold water and dry on kitchen paper towels. Put 1 teaspoon of the mustard inside each fish and spread out evenly. Season.

Butter three pieces of foil large enough to wrap the fish in, and place a fish in the centre of each. Dot with a little butter and seal. Put on a baking tray (cookie sheet) and bake in the oven at 375°F/190°C/Gas 5 for about 30 minutes (depending on size) or until the fish are tender.

Either serve the fish in their parcels or remove and serve on a bed of hot brown rice tossed with cooked chopped onion, mushrooms and herbs. Garnish with lemon and parsley.

Serves 3

Chicken Risotto

This filling and fairly fat-free dish is delicious served either hot or cold with a fresh green salad.

Imperial/metric	American
4 oz (100 g) brown rice	½ cup brown rice
4 oz (100 g) long-grain rice	½ cup long-grain rice
1½ oz (40 g) polyunsaturated margarine	3 tablespoons margarine
1 onion, chopped	1 onion, chopped
3 sticks celery, chopped	3 stalks celery, chopped
12 oz (350 g) chicken breast (about 3), skinned and boned, cut into 3 inch (7.5 cm) long pencil strips	3 chicken breasts, skinned, boned and cut into 3 inch long pencil strips
4 oz (100 g) mushrooms, sliced	1 cup sliced mushrooms
4 oz (100 g) canned sweetcorn, drained	¾ cup cooked corn
14 oz (397 g) can peeled tomatoes	1½ cups canned tomatoes
2 tablespoons freshly chopped parsley	2 tablespoons freshly chopped parsley
salt and freshly ground black pepper	salt and freshly ground black pepper

Cook the rices separately, in plenty of boiling salted water, until just tender. Rinse well under running cold water and drain thoroughly.

Heat the margarine in a large pan, fry onion and celery for about 10 minutes until browned, then add the chicken and cook for a further 10 minutes until the chicken is tender. Stir in the mushrooms, drained sweetcorn, tomatoes, rice, parsley and seasoning, and mix well until thoroughly blended. Cook gently until piping hot, stirring occasionally to prevent it from sticking.

Serves 4

Roast Chicken with Wild Rice Stuffing

It is possible to buy packets of mixed long-grain and wild rice in most supermarkets and health-food shops. (Wild rice, incidentally, *isn't* a rice, but a grass, and it's harvested by North American Indians!)

Imperial/metric	American
6 fl. oz (175 ml) fresh orange juice	¾ cup fresh orange juice
2 oz (50 g) long-grain and wild rice mixture	½ cup mixed long-grain and wild rice
2 oz (50 g) polyunsaturated margarine	¼ cup margarine
1 small onion, finely chopped	1 small onion, finely chopped
2 sticks celery, finely chopped	2 stalks celery, finely chopped
1 oz (25 g) blanched almonds, chopped	¼ cup blanched almonds, chopped
2 oz (50 g) dried apricots, soaked overnight and chopped	½ cup dried apricots, soaked overnight and chopped
2 tablespoons freshly chopped parsley	2 tablespoons freshly chopped parsley
salt and freshly ground black pepper	salt and freshly ground black pepper
4 lb (1.8 kg) fresh chicken	4 lb fresh chicken

Heat the oven to 375°F/190°C/Gas 5.

Bring the orange juice to the boil in a saucepan. Stir in rice, cover with a lid and simmer gently for about 20 minutes then leave on one side for about 5 minutes so the rice can absorb the remaining liquid.

Heat half of the margarine and quickly sauté onion and celery for about 5 minutes until soft. Lift off heat and stir in almonds, apricots, parsley, seasoning and rice.

Remove giblets from chicken and use for stock for gravy. Stuff the neck end of the bird with the rice stuffing and secure skin firmly over stuffing with small skewers (wooden picks) (push into shape with the hands). Spread chicken with remaining margarine, season and roast in the oven for about 1½ hours until the chicken is cooked. To test when done, pierce the thigh of the bird and if the juices that run out are clear then the chicken is cooked.

Allow chicken to rest for a few minutes before carving.

Serves 6

Sesame Chicken

The children in particular will enjoy these chicken thighs. I sometimes pack them up in a lunchbox or take them on a picnic. Sesame seeds are rich in magnesium, potassium and calcium as well as being a good source of Vitamin E.

Imperial/metric	American
6 chicken thighs, skinned	6 chicken thighs, skinned
2 tablespoons sunflower oil	2 tablespoons sunflower oil
3 oz (75 g) sesame seeds	½ cup sesame seeds
freshly ground black pepper	freshly ground black pepper

Brush the chicken thighs with oil then roll in the sesame seeds. You may have to repeat this process to get a good coating of seeds.

Season with pepper then cook under a hot grill (broiler) for about 25 minutes until the chicken is tender, turning the thighs constantly during cooking. Serve either hot or cold.

Serves 6

Country Chicken

A colourful dish, which is delicious served with a fresh green vegetable such as broccoli.

Imperial/metric	American
1 tablespoon sunflower oil	*1 tablespoon sunflower oil*
knob of polyunsaturated margarine	*1 tablespoon margarine*
1 onion, sliced	*1 onion, sliced*
4 chicken breasts, skinned and boned	*4 chicken breasts, skinned and boned*
8 tomatoes	*8 tomatoes*
salt and freshly ground black pepper	*salt and freshly ground black pepper*
juice of ½ lemon	*juice of ½ lemon*
freshly chopped parsley	*freshly chopped parsley*

Heat the oil and margarine in a pan (large skillet) and fry onion for about 5 minutes until soft then add the chicken breasts and cook until browned all over.

Skin the tomatoes by plunging them in boiling water for a minute and then peeling off the skin. Slice tomatoes and arrange in the bottom of a 2 pint/1.2 litre (5 cup) ovenproof dish. Lift the onion and chicken breasts on top. Season well with salt and pepper and pour lemon juice on top.

Cover with a piece of foil then bake in the oven at 400°F/200°C/Gas 6 for about 25 minutes until the chicken is tender. Serve sprinkled with a little freshly chopped parsley.

Serves 4

Stir Fry Chicken

Stir frying is an extremely quick method of cooking. The food keeps its texture and loses little food value.

Imperial/metric	American
4 tablespoons sunflower oil	4 tablespoons sunflower oil
3 chicken breasts, skinned, boned and cut into thin strips	3 chicken breasts, skinned, boned and cut into thin strips
4 spring onions, chopped	4 scallions, chopped
1 teaspoon finely chopped fresh root ginger	1 teaspoon finely chopped fresh root ginger
1 fat clove garlic, crushed	1 whole clove garlic, crushed
2 oz (50 g) unsalted cashew nuts	⅓ cup unsalted cashew nuts
4 oz (100 g) beansprouts	2 cups beansprouts
salt and freshly ground black pepper	salt and freshly ground black pepper
4 level teaspoons cornflour	4 level teaspoons cornstarch
4 tablespoons sherry	4 tablespoons sherry
1 tablespoon soy sauce	1 tablespoon soy sauce
1 tablespoon freshly chopped parsley	1 tablespoon freshly chopped parsley
wedges of lime or lemon to garnish	wedges of lime or lemon to garnish

Heat the oil in a large deep frying pan or in a wok until very hot. Add the strips of chicken, spring onions (scallions), ginger and garlic and toss well in the oil for about 5 minutes.

Add the nuts, beansprouts and salt and pepper to taste and continue to cook for a few more moments.

Slake the cornflour (cornstarch) with the sherry and add to the pan with the soy sauce and parsley. Continue to stir fry for a further 2 minutes, then spoon onto a warmed serving dish, decorate with lime or lemon wedges and serve with cooked brown rice.

Serves 4

Chicken Parcels

These can be baked on a barbecue rather than in the oven if preferred. Be sure, however, that the chicken is thoroughly cooked. Serve with a crunchy colourful salad.

Imperial/metric

4 chicken portions
4 oz (100 g) bacon pieces, chopped
4 oz (100 g) mushrooms, sliced
2 oz (50 g) onion, finely chopped
salt and freshly ground black pepper

American

4 chicken portions
½ cup chopped bacon
1 cup sliced mushrooms
½ cup chopped onion
salt and freshly ground black pepper

Heat the oven to 200°C/400°F/Gas 6.

Skin the pieces of chicken and remove any fat. Cut four pieces of foil large enough to wrap the chicken joints in, and stand a chicken portion on each.

Cook the bacon in a non-stick pan (skillet) over a low heat until the fat begins to run out, then increase heat, add the mushrooms and onion, and fry for about 5 minutes until the onion is tender. Season the chicken portions with salt and pepper and spoon a little of the bacon mixture on top of each piece of chicken. Wrap securely in the foil, lift onto a baking tray (cookie tray), and cook in the oven for about 40 minutes until the chicken is tender.

To serve, either lift out of parcels or keep still wrapped in the foil with the top opened up.

Serves 4

Venison in Beer

Stewing venison is inexpensive, but often difficult to get hold of. I tend to buy 6 lb (2.75 kg) at a time, and freeze the rest until I need it. As it's very lean, venison keeps in the freezer up to 6 months, and is very useful for pies and casseroles.

Imperial/metric

1½ lb (675 g) stewing venison, cubed
2 tablespoons sunflower oil
2 medium onions, chopped
½ oz (15 g) flour
¾ pint (450 ml) beer
1 sprig thyme
1 bay leaf
1 teaspoon muscovado sugar
salt and freshly ground black pepper

American

1½ lb stewing venison, cubed
2 tablespoons sunflower oil
2 medium sized onions, chopped
2 tablespoons all-purpose flour
2 cups beer
1 sprig thyme
1 bay leaf
1 teaspoon light brown sugar
salt and freshly ground black pepper

Brown the meat on all sides by quickly frying in the oil which has been heated in a non-stick pan (skillet). Lift meat out with a slotted spoon and leave on one side. Add the onion to the juices left in the pan and fry until golden. Blend in the flour and cook for a minute. Remove the pan from the heat, and gradually blend in the beer. Bring to the boil, stirring until thickened slightly. Return the meat to the pan with the thyme, bay leaf, sugar and seasoning.

Cover the pan with a lid and simmer gently for about 2 hours until the venison is tender. Check seasoning, remove thyme and bay leaf, and serve with plain boiled potatoes to sop up the thinnish sauce.

Serves 6

Pheasant with Port and Orange

One good sized pheasant usually serves four people. The cooking time will vary with the age of the bird: a young one would only take an hour.

Imperial/metric

1 casserole pheasant
a little polyunsaturated
  margarine
salt and freshly ground black
  pepper

Sauce

2 tablespoons pheasant fat (see
  method)
1 oz (25 g) plain flour
4 fl. oz (100 ml) port
½ pint (300 ml) good stock
2 large oranges
1 tablespoon redcurrant jelly

American

1 casserole pheasant
a little margarine
salt and freshly ground black
  pepper

Sauce

2 tablespoons pheasant fat (see
  method)
¼ cup all-purpose flour
½ cup port
1¼ cups good stock
2 large sweet oranges
1 tablespoon redcurrant jelly

Heat the oven to 400°F/200°C/Gas 6.

Rub the pheasant with a small amount of margarine and season well with salt and pepper. Place in a roasting tin and roast for about 1½–2 hours until tender.

Remove from the oven and pour any inside juices into a measuring jug. Skim off and retain all the fat from the roasting tin, and add any juices to those in the jug. Place the pheasant on a warm serving dish and keep warm.

Put 2 tablespoons of the pheasant fat in a saucepan, add flour and cook for a minute, then gradually blend in the port. Make the juices from the bird up to ½ pint/300 ml (1¼ cups) with stock and add this to the pan. Bring to the boil, stirring until thickened. Season to taste, then simmer for about 5 minutes allowing the sauce to reduce slightly.

Thinly peel one orange, shred the peel finely and simmer for 3 minutes in a little water. Drain well. Squeeze the juice from 1½ oranges and cut the remaining unpeeled half in slices for garnish. Add the orange juice and redcurrant jelly to the saucepan and stir until jelly has dissolved. Taste and check seasoning.

Carve the bird and sprinkle each serving with the orange rind and garnish with the orange slices. Serve sauce separately.

Serves 4

Spicy Lamb with Rice

When you have a little meat left from the Sunday roast this is an excellent way of using it up. You could, of course, use fresh vegetables, but be sure that they're varied and that they're cut up small so that they stir-fry quickly.

Imperial/metric	American
8 oz (225 g) brown rice	1 cup brown rice
1 tablespoon sunflower oil	1 tablespoon sunflower oil
2 medium onions, sliced	2 medium onions, sliced
8 oz (225 g) packet frozen mixed vegetables, thawed	1½ cups frozen mixed vegetables, thawed
3 tablespoons soy sauce	3 tablespoons soy sauce
1 tablespoon Worcestershire sauce	1 tablespoon Worcestershire sauce
1 level teaspoon curry powder	1 teaspoon curry powder
salt and freshly ground black pepper	salt and freshly ground black pepper
8–12 oz (225–350 g) cooked lean lamb, diced	1–1½ cups diced cooked lean lamb

Cook the rice in plenty of boiling salted water until just tender as directed on the packet. Drain and rinse well.

Heat the oil in a pan and fry onion for about 5 minutes until soft. Stir the mixed vegetables into the saucepan with the rice, soy and Worcestershire sauces, curry powder, seasoning and lamb. Heat through, stirring continuously until thoroughly mixed and piping hot. Turn into a warmed serving dish to serve.

Serves 4

Lamb with Apricots

Serve this dish with plain boiled rice or noodles. Apricots are particularly rich in Vitamin A (and when fresh aren't available, use dried, but soak them overnight first).

Imperial/metric	American
1½ lb (675 g) lean stewing lamb	1½ lb lean stewing lamb
1 tablespoon sunflower oil	1 tablespoon sunflower oil
1 large onion, chopped	1 large onion, chopped
2 level teaspoons paprika pepper	2 level teaspoons paprika pepper
1 oz (25 g) flour	¼ cup all-purpose flour
½ pint (300 ml) good stock	1¼ cups good stock
salt and freshly ground black pepper	salt and freshly ground black pepper
1 teaspoon light muscovado sugar	1 teaspoon light brown sugar
1 tablespoon white wine vinegar	1 tablespoon white wine vinegar
8 oz (225 g) fresh apricots	2 fresh apricots
4 oz (100 g) frozen peas	1 cup frozen peas

Cut the meat into neat bite-sized pieces. Heat the oil in a saucepan and quickly fry onion for about 5 minutes until soft, then add the meat and continue to cook until browned all over. Stir in the paprika and flour and cook for a minute. Gradually blend in the stock, seasoning, sugar and vinegar and bring to the boil, stirring until thickened. Simmer with a lid for about 1 hour until the meat is just tender.

Stone (seed) and quarter the apricots and add to the meat. Cook for about 30 more minutes, adding the peas for the last 15 minutes of cooking. Taste and check seasoning then turn into a serving dish.

Serves 4

Scotch Broth Stew

This dish is a cross between a soup and a stew. It is very warming to serve on a cold winter's day. The dried soup mix is the sort with lentils, split peas etc and needs soaking before it is added. It can be bought in cellophane packets at good supermarkets and health-food shops.

Imperial/metric	American
8 oz (225 g) carrots, sliced	2 large carrots, sliced
6 pieces middle end neck lamb, trimmed of fat	6 pieces middle end neck lamb, trimmed of fat
2 oz (50 g) dried soup mix, soaked overnight	½ cup dried soup mix, soaked overnight
1½ pints (900 ml) good light chicken stock	3¾ cups good light chicken stock
salt and freshly ground black pepper	salt and freshly ground black pepper
1 lb (450 g) potatoes, thinly peeled and sliced	1 lb potatoes, thinly peeled and sliced

Heat the oven to 350°F/180°C/Gas 4.

Arrange the carrots in the bottom of a 2½ pint/1.5 litre (6¼ cup) ovenproof dish, then arrange the pieces of lamb on top. Sprinkle with soaked soup mix, pour over stock and season well. Arrange slices of potato on top of meat to completely cover dish.

Cover with a lid and cook for an hour in the oven then remove the lid and cook for about another hour until the meat is tender and the potatoes are beginning to brown. Serve straight from the oven, and there's no need for extra vegetables.

Serves 3

Minted Lamb Chops

Lamb chops are delicious when cooked simply and healthily in this way.

Imperial/metric	American
4 lamb chops, trimmed of fat	*4 lamb chops, trimmed of fat*
mint jelly	*mint jelly*
4 oz (100 g) button mushrooms	*1 cup button mushrooms*
sprigs of watercress to garnish	*sprigs of watercress to garnish*

Heat the grill (broiler) to moderate. Arrange the chops in the grill (broiler) pan, spread a little mint jelly on the top of each, then grill (broil) for about 8 minutes. Turn the chops over and glaze again with the mint jelly.

Add the mushrooms to the grill (broiler) pan and toss in the juices which have run out of the meat, then grill (broil) for about 8 more minutes until the chops are brown. Lift out and arrange on a serving plate with the mushrooms, and garnish with sprigs of watercress. Serve with fresh green broccoli.

Serves 4

Lamb Noisettes

These are excellent either grilled (broiled) or cooked on a barbecue.

Imperial/metric	American
6 cutlet pieces best end neck of lamb	6 cutlet pieces best end neck of lamb
salt and freshly ground black pepper	salt and freshly ground black pepper
a little dried rosemary	a little dried rosemary
3 lamb's kidneys	3 lamb kidneys
6 rashers streaky bacon	6 slices bacon

Ask the butcher to bone the piece of lamb for you, or to do this yourself. Cut off the chine bone at the thick end of the joint. Using a sharp pointed knife, cut along either side of each bone and ease out. Trim all excess fat from the meat.

Season well and sprinkle meat with rosemary. Remove skin and cores from the kidneys and lay along the width of the meat. Roll up lengthwise. Cut the joint into six even slices, wrap a rasher of bacon around each slice, and secure with a piece of fine string and small skewers to prevent the kidney from coming out during cooking.

Grill (broil) for about 15 minutes under a hot grill or over hot barbecue coals, turning once during cooking until clear juices run out from the meat.

Serves 6

Rack of Lamb with Plum Sauce

This sauce goes particularly well with lamb and makes a special Sunday roast.

Imperial/metric	American
2 racks best end neck of lamb, chined (each rack with about 6 cutlets)	2 racks of lamb, chined
1 lb (450 g) plums, stoned	1 lb red plums, seeded
3 oz (75 g) light muscovado sugar	6 tablespoons firmly packed light brown sugar
2 tablespoons water	2 tablespoons water
4 tablespoons inexpensive sherry	4 tablespoons inexpensive sherry
4 tablespoons redcurrant jelly	4 tablespoons redcurrant jelly
watercress to garnish	watercress to garnish

Heat the oven to 400°F/200°C/Gas 6.

Mark a straight line across the racks of lamb about 1 inch (2.5 cm) from the tops of the ribs. Remove the meat and fat from between the ribs above this line, then join the racks together so that the ribs link at the top with the skin facing the outside. Secure with string. Lift into a roasting tin (pan) and roast in the preheated oven for about an hour until the meat is tender and the outside browned and crispy. Remove string and keep meat warm on a serving dish.

For the sauce, put the plums in a saucepan with the sugar and water and simmer gently for about 20 minutes until the plums are tender. Pour into a processor or blender and reduce to a purée. Blend the sherry and redcurrant jelly into the sauce, return to the saucepan and reheat gently until jelly has melted and the sauce is hot. Pour into a warmed sauce boat and serve separately with the lamb, garnished with watercress.

Serves 6

Apple and Pork Churdles

These make a very tasty hot lunch, served with apple jelly. They can also be served cold and taken on a picnic or included in a packed lunch. Pork *is* fatty, but the acidity of the apple – the traditional accompaniment – counteracts this (as well as adding considerably to the flavour).

Imperial/metric	American
1 tablespoon sunflower oil	1 tablespoon sunflower oil
1 small onion, chopped	1 small onion, chopped
2 oz (50 g) button mushrooms, sliced	½ cup sliced button mushrooms
1 medium Bramley apple, peeled, cored and chopped	1 medium sized cooking apple, peeled, cored and chopped
8 oz (225 g) raw, lean pork, minced	1 cup firmly packed raw ground pork
1 tablespoon freshly chopped parsley	1 tablespoon freshly chopped parsley
salt and freshly ground black pepper	salt and freshly ground black pepper

Pastry	Pastry
6 oz (175 g) self-raising flour	1½ cups self-rising flour
2 oz (50 g) wholemeal flour	½ cup wholewheat flour
2 oz (50 g) lard	¼ cup shortening
2 oz (50 g) polyunsaturated margarine	¼ cup margarine
about 2 good tablespoons water	about 2 good tablespoons water
4 oz (100 g) mature Cheddar cheese, grated	1 cup grated aged Cheddar cheese
a little beaten egg to glaze	a little beaten egg to glaze

Heat the oven to 350°F/180°C/Gas 4.

Start by preparing the filling. Heat the oil in a pan (skillet) and quickly fry onion for about 5 minutes until soft. Add the mushrooms and apple and cook for a few more minutes until the apple is beginning to soften. Lift from pan (skillet) with a slotted spoon into a bowl. Fry the meat in the juices left in the pan (skillet) for about 10 minutes, then add to the apple mixture in the bowl with the parsley and seasoning. Leave to cool.

For the pastry, measure the flours into a bowl, rub in fats until mixture resembles fine breadcrumbs then mix to a dough with the water. Rest dough in fridge for 15 minutes if time allows. Turn dough out onto a lightly floured surface, and knead gently until smooth. Roll out and cut into 6 inch (15 cm) rounds.

Pile the apple mixture in the centre of each pastry round, brush edges with a little water then pull up sides so that they almost meet, leaving a hole in the top. Sprinkle the cheese on top of this hole. Brush with a little beaten egg. Bake in the oven on a baking tray (cookie sheet) for about 30 minutes until the pastry is cooked and the cheese has melted and is a golden brown.

Makes about 6 churdles

Marinated Pork Kebabs

These can be either cooked under the grill (broiler) or on a barbecue. Cooking them on a barbecue always makes them seem that bit more special. By grilling, of course, much of the hidden fat – even in the lean fillet – drips out.

Imperial/metric

1 lb (450 g) fillet of pork
4 firm tomatoes, halved
16 button mushrooms
1 red pepper, seeded and cut
  into squares
salt and freshly ground black
  pepper

Marinade

2 tablespoons sunflower oil
1 tablespoon white wine vinegar
2 cloves of garlic, crushed
salt and freshly ground black
  pepper

American

1 lb fillet of pork
4 firm tomatoes, halved
16 button mushrooms
1 red pepper, seeded and cut
  into squares
salt and freshly ground black
  pepper

Marinade

2 tablespoons sunflower oil
1 tablespoon white wine vinegar
2 cloves of garlic, crushed
salt and freshly ground black
  pepper

Cut the pork into neat bite-sized pieces. Blend all the marinade ingredients together in a bowl, and stir in the pork. Cover with clingfilm (plastic wrap) and then refrigerate overnight.

Preheat the grill (broiler) or barbeque when you wish to cook.

Thread the pork, tomatoes, mushrooms and pieces of pepper alternately onto four long flat skewers. Season lightly then grill (broil) or barbecue for about 15 minutes until the pork is tender. Keep brushing the kebabs with the marinade during cooking, and turn them too. Put the kebabs onto a warm serving dish and serve with a green salad.

Serves 4

Langham Beef Casserole

This is a special casserole, ideal to serve with a delicious crisp green vegetable like broccoli spears when you have friends for supper on a winter's evening.

Imperial/metric	American
1 tablespoon sunflower oil	*1 tablespoon sunflower oil*
2 lb (900 g) lean stewing steak, cubed	*2 lb lean stewing steak, cubed*
1 large onion, sliced	*1 large onion, sliced*
3 large carrots, sliced	*3 large carrots, sliced*
1 oz (25 g) flour	*¼ cup all-purpose flour*
½ pint (300 ml) good stock	*1¼ cups good stock*
¼ pint (150 ml) inexpensive red wine or port	*⅔ cup inexpensive red wine or port*
2 teaspoons redcurrant jelly	*2 teaspoons redcurrant jelly*
salt and freshly ground black pepper	*salt and freshly ground black pepper*
dash of gravy browning	*dash gravy coloring*

Heat the oven to 350°F/180°C/Gas 4.

Heat the oil in a pan (skillet) and quickly fry meat until browned all over. Transfer to a 2½ pint/1.5 litre (6¼ cup) casserole dish with a slotted spoon, then add the onion and carrot to the juices left in the pan. Quickly fry until the onion is tender and the carrot a bright orange colour. Stir in the flour and cook for a minute then gradually blend in the stock and wine. Bring to the boil, stirring until thickened, then add the redcurrant jelly, seasoning and a dash of gravy browning (colouring)

Pour over the meat in the casserole, cover with a lid, and cook in the oven for about 2 hours until the meat is tender. Taste and check seasoning then serve immediately.

Serves 4–6

Meatballs
in Peppered Sauce

These meatballs are economical to prepare, as the bread helps to eke out the meat. Serve with a lightly cooked green vegetable.

Imperial/metric

1 large onion, finely chopped
1 lb (450 g) lean minced beef
4 oz (100 g) fresh brown
    breadcrumbs
grated rind and juice of 1 lemon
salt and freshly ground black
    pepper
sunflower oil to fry

Sauce

½ oz (15 g) butter
1 small onion, finely chopped
1 tablespoon paprika pepper
½ pint (300 ml) good stock
4 oz (100 g) mushrooms,
    roughly chopped
8 oz (225 g) can peeled
    tomatoes
1 tablespoon tomato purée
1 tablespoon white wine vinegar
1½ tablespoons dark muscovado
    sugar
salt

American

1 large onion, finely chopped
2 cups firmly packed raw
    ground beef
2 cups fresh soft brown
    breadcrumbs
grated rind and juice of 1 lemon
salt and freshly ground black
    pepper
sunflower oil to fry

Sauce

1 tablespoon butter
1 small onion, finely chopped
1 tablespoon paprika pepper
1¼ cups good stock
1 cup roughly chopped
    mushrooms
1 cup canned tomatoes
1 tablespoon tomato purée
1 tablespoon white wine vinegar
1½ tablespoons dark brown
    sugar
salt

Start by preparing the meatballs. Cook the onion in boiling water for about 10 minutes until tender, drain thoroughly, then allow to cool. Put onion in a bowl with the minced (ground) beef, breadcrumbs, lemon rind and juice and seasoning. Mix well until thoroughly blended. Divide into sixteen pieces, and shape into balls with lightly floured hands. Chill in the refrigerator for about 3 hours until really cold, and preheat the oven to 350°F/180°C/Gas 4.

For the sauce, heat the butter in a pan (skillet) and fry onion for about 10 minutes until golden brown. Stir in the remaining ingredients. Bring to the boil, cover with a lid and simmer gently for about 20 minutes. Allow to cool slightly then reduce to a purée in a processor or blender. Taste and check seasoning and transfer to a 2 pint/1.2 litre (5 cup) shallow ovenproof dish.

Heat sunflower oil in a pan (skillet) and fry meatballs for about 10 minutes until browned all over. Drain well on kitchen paper towels then arrange on top of the sauce. Cook in the oven for about 40 minutes until the meatballs are tender and the sauce is bubbling.

Serves 4

Chilli Con Carne

This is always an interesting – and healthy – dish to make. The beans are a good source of fibre and minerals, and help pad out the meat.

Chilli powders and seasonings vary considerably in spiciness between different brands, so be sure to check carefully and adjust accordingly. Try serving the chilli with brown, rather than white, rice for a change.

Imperial/metric	American
4 oz (100 g) bacon pieces, chopped	½ cup chopped bacon
1 large onion, chopped	1 large onion, chopped
2 sticks celery, sliced	2 stalks celery, sliced
2 fat cloves of garlic, crushed	2 whole fat cloves of garlic, crushed
1½ lb (675 g) lean minced beef	3 cups firmly packed lean ground beef
1 oz (25 g) flour	¼ cup all-purpose flour
2¼ oz (63 g) can tomato purée	¼ cup tomato purée
1 pint (600 ml) good beef stock	2½ cups good beef stock
salt and freshly ground black pepper	salt and freshly ground black pepper
1 teaspoon chilli seasoning	1 teaspoon chilli seasoning
15 oz (425 g) can red kidney beans, drained	1 cup canned red kidney beans, drained
1 green pepper, cored, seeded and chopped	1 green pepper, cored, seeded and chopped

Gently cook the bacon in a large non-stick pan (skillet) until fat begins to run out, then increase the heat and fry for about 5 minutes. Add the onion, celery and garlic and continue to cook until the onion is a golden brown. Add the minced (ground) beef and cook for about 5 minutes until browned all over. Stir in the flour and cook for a minute then blend in purée and stock. Bring to the boil, stirring until thickened.

Add the seasoning, then simmer gently for about 1½ hours until the minced beef is tender. Add the beans and green pepper for the last half-hour of cooking time. Taste and check seasoning and serve immediately.

Serves 6

Home-made Beefburgers

These are so much better for you than the commercially bought ones and are very simple to prepare. Serve as a snack in a warmed wholemeal or granary roll (see page 170), with a little salad for extra goodness.

Imperial/metric	American
8 oz (225 g) onion, chopped	2 cups chopped onion
12 oz (350 g) very lean, raw, minced beef	1½ cups raw ground beef, firmly packed
2 oz (50 g) fresh brown breadcrumbs	1 cup fresh soft brown breadcrumbs
1 egg, beaten	1 egg, beaten
2 tablespoons freshly chopped parsley	2 tablespoons freshly chopped parsley
salt and freshly ground black pepper	salt and freshly ground black pepper

Cook the onion in boiling salted water for about 5 minutes until tender then drain well. Put the onion in a bowl, add the minced beef, breadcrumbs, egg, parsley and seasoning.

Mix well until the mixture is thoroughly blended. Divide the mixture into eight. With lightly floured hands shape the mixture into balls and then flatten to form a burger shape. Chill in the refrigerator for about 5 hours before cooking.

Heat the grill (broiler) and grill burgers for about 15 minutes until cooked through, turning once during cooking.

Makes 8 burgers

Lasagne

I use the wholewheat lasagne that you do not have to pre-cook, as it saves a great deal of time and washing-up too! Again, this is a meal complete in itself, but a crisp green salad wouldn't go amiss.

Imperial/metric	American
2 oz (50 g) streaky bacon, derinded and chopped	¼ cup chopped bacon
1½ lb (675 g) lean minced beef	3 cups firmly packed raw ground beef
8 oz (225 g) onion, chopped	2 cups chopped onion
3 sticks celery, chopped	3 stalks celery, chopped
½ oz (15 g) flour	2 tablespoons all-purpose flour
¾ pint (450 ml) good stock	2 cups good stock
3 tablespoons tomato purée	3 tablespoons tomato purée
2 fat cloves of garlic, crushed	2 whole fat cloves of garlic, crushed
salt and freshly ground black pepper	salt and freshly ground black pepper
¼ teaspoon mixed dried herbs	¼ teaspoon mixed dried herbs

White sauce	White sauce
1½ oz (40 g) polyunsaturated margarine	3 tablespoons margarine
1½ oz (40 g) flour	5 tablespoons all-purpose flour
pinch of ground nutmeg	pinch of ground nutmeg
salt and freshly ground black pepper	salt and freshly ground black pepper
1 pint (600 ml) skimmed milk	2½ cups skim milk
¼ teaspoon made mustard	¼ teaspoon mustard
5 oz (150 g) uncooked wholewheat lasagne	5 oz uncooked wholewheat lasagne
8 oz (225 g) mature Cheddar cheese, grated	2 cups grated aged Cheddar cheese

For the meat sauce, gently fry the bacon in a non-stick pan (skillet) until fat begins to run out then increase heat, add minced (ground) beef and fry until browned all over. Add onion and celery and cook for a few more minutes until onion is soft. Stir in the flour, stock, purée, garlic, seasoning and herbs, and bring to the boil, stirring until thickened. Cover with a lid and simmer for about an hour until the meat is tender, stirring occasionally to prevent the sauce from sticking.

For the white sauce, melt the margarine in a saucepan, stir in the flour, nutmeg, salt and pepper and cook for a minute, then gradually blend in the milk. Bring to the boil, stirring until thickened. Stir in mustard then taste and check seasoning.

In a shallow 4 pint/2.25 litre (10 cup) ovenproof dish put a third of the meat sauce, a third of the white sauce and a third of the cheese. On top of this arrange half the lasagne, laying the sheets edge to edge without overlapping. Repeat in layers until finishing with a final layer of cheese on top. Allow to become cold.

When required, cook in the oven at 350°F/180°C/Gas 4 for about 45 minutes until piping hot and the cheese is golden brown and bubbling.

Serves 6

Beefy Meatloaf

This is a particular favourite with the children. Serve in slices with a fresh green or mixed salad, or with creamed potato and a green vegetable. If there is any meatloaf left, it can always be sliced and used to fill pitta bread with some salad for lunch.

Imperial/metric	American
1 lb (450 g) lean minced beef	2 cups firmly packed ground beef
3 oz (75 g) fresh brown breadcrumbs	1½ cups fresh soft brown breadcrumbs
1 medium onion, coarsely grated	1 medium sized onion, coarsely grated
2 carrots, grated	2 carrots, grated
1 egg, lightly beaten	1 egg, lightly beaten
salt and freshly ground black pepper	salt and freshly ground black pepper
2 tablespoons freshly chopped parsley	2 tablespoons freshly chopped parsley

Heat the oven to 350°F/180°C/Gas 4.

Mix all the ingredients together in a bowl until thoroughly blended. Press down firmly into a 1 lb (450 g) loaf tin (pan) and level the top.

Bake in the oven for about 1¼ hours until the loaf is cooked (juices should run out clear from the loaf when tested with a skewer or wooden pick. Turn out onto a serving dish and serve warm with vegetables or cold with salad.

Serves 4

Macaroni Cheese with Mushrooms

This is a meal in itself – a good combination of incomplete protein (the grain in the pasta), the complete protein of the cheese, and the vegetable goodness of the mushrooms – but if the family are particularly hungry, serve with fresh wholewheat granary rolls (see page 170).

Imperial/metric	American
6 oz (175 g) short-cut wholemeal macaroni	1½ cups raw wholewheat macaroni
2 oz (50 g) polyunsaturated margarine	¼ cup margarine
1 small onion, chopped	1 small onion, chopped
4 oz (100 g) mushrooms, sliced	1 cup sliced mushrooms
2 oz (50 g) flour	½ cup all-purpose flour
1½ pints (900 ml) skimmed milk	3¾ cups skim milk
salt and freshly ground black pepper	salt and freshly ground black pepper
3 oz (75 g) well flavoured Cheddar cheese, grated	¾ cup grated aged Cheddar cheese

Heat the oven to 425°F/220°C/Gas 7. Lightly grease a 2½ pint/1.5 litre (6¼ cup) ovenproof dish.

Cook the macaroni in boiling salted water as directed by the manufacturers on the side of the packet. Drain well.

Melt the margarine in a saucepan and fry onion for about 10 minutes until golden brown, then add the mushrooms and cook for a few moments. Stir in the flour and cook for a minute, then gradually blend in milk. Bring to the boil, stirring until thickened. Season to taste and stir in the macaroni. Turn the mixture into the prepared dish and sprinkle the cheese on top.

Cook in the oven until the sauce is bubbling and the cheese has melted. Serve hot straight from the oven.

Serves 4

Savoury Cheese Crumble

This dish is ideal when you are planning to go out for the day and want something that just needs heating when you get back. Serve with fresh green vegetables – which only take moments to prepare and cook.

Imperial/metric

1 lb (450 g) lean minced beef
1 large onion, finely chopped
1 oz (25 g) flour
¾ pint (450 ml) good beef stock
salt and freshly ground black pepper
dash of Worcestershire sauce
2 carrots, grated

Topping
2 oz (50 g) self-raising flour
2 oz (50 g) wholemeal flour
1 oz (25 g) polyunsaturated margarine
2 oz (50 g) mature Cheddar cheese, grated
salt and freshly ground black pepper
½ teaspoon dry mustard powder
2 tomatoes, sliced

American

2 cups firmly packed ground beef
1 large onion, finely chopped
¼ cup all-purpose flour
2 cups good beef stock
salt and freshly ground black pepper
dash of Worcestershire sauce
2 carrots, grated

Topping
½ cup self-rising flour
½ cup wholewheat flour
2 tablespoons margarine
½ cup aged Cheddar cheese, grated
salt and freshly ground black pepper
½ teaspoon dried mustard
2 tomatoes, sliced

Put the minced (ground) beef in a non-stick saucepan and heat gently until fat begins to run out, then increase heat and fry quickly until browned all over. Add onion and fry until soft, then stir in flour. Cook for a minute then gradually blend in stock, and bring to the boil, stirring until thickened.

Season with salt and pepper, add Worcestershire sauce and carrot, then cover with a lid and simmer for about 45 minutes until the mince is tender. Taste and check seasoning then turn into a 2½ pint/1.5 litre (6¼ cup) ovenproof dish.

For the topping, measure the flours into a bowl and rub in margarine until mixture resembles fine breadcrumbs. Stir in the cheese, seasoning and mustard. Spoon over the top of the mince (ground beef).

Cook in the oven at 350°F/180°C/Gas 4 for about 50 minutes until the topping is crisp and a golden brown, adding the slices of tomato for the last 10 minutes cooking time.

Serves 4

Liver and Tomato Casserole

This is a colourful casserole, ideal for a quick midweek supper. Liver is rich in many minerals, especially iron, and the Vitamin C of the tomatoes will aid its ingestion. For best health, try to serve liver once a week.

Imperial/metric	American
4 oz (100 g) bacon pieces, chopped	½ cup chopped bacon
1 onion, chopped	1 onion, chopped
1 lb (450 g) pig's liver, sliced	1 lb pork liver, sliced
1 oz (25 g) flour	¼ cup all-purpose flour
14 oz (397 g) can peeled tomatoes	1½ cups canned tomatoes
½ pint (300 ml) good beef stock	1¼ cups good beef stock
1 tablespoon tomato purée	1 tablespoon tomato purée
4 oz (100 g) button mushrooms, sliced	1 cup sliced button mushrooms
salt and freshly ground black pepper	salt and freshly ground black pepper

Heat the oven to 350°F/180°C/Gas 4.

Gently cook the bacon pieces in a non-stick pan (skillet) until the fat begins to run out, then add onion. Increase heat and fry until the onion is tender. Add the liver to the pan (skillet) and fry until browned all over. Lift the liver out of the pan (skillet) with a slotted spoon and arrange in a 2 pint/1.2 litre (5 cup) ovenproof dish.

Add the flour to the onion and bacon left in the pan (skillet) and cook for a minute then gradually blend in the tomatoes and stock. Bring to the boil, stirring until thickened, then add the purée, mushrooms and seasoning.

Pour the sauce over the liver, cover the dish with foil, and cook in the oven for about 45 minutes until the liver is tender. Serve with brown rice.

Serves 4

Devilled Kidneys

Kidneys, too, like most offal, are rich in nutrients. Serve with boiled brown rice to mop up the rich sauce, and a green vegetable.

Imperial/metric	American
12 pickling onions	12 baby onions
8 lamb's kidneys	8 lamb kidneys
4 oz (100 g) bacon pieces, roughly chopped	½ cup chopped bacon
1 oz (25 g) flour	¼ cup all-purpose flour
¼ pint (150 ml) red wine	⅔ cup red wine
¼ pint (150 ml) good beef stock	⅔ cup good beef stock
1 tablespoon tomato purée	1 tablespoon tomato purée
salt and freshly ground black pepper	salt and freshly ground black pepper

Peel the onions and trim off the top and bottom of the onions – but leave them whole. Put in a saucepan, cover with water and bring to the boil. Simmer for about 5 minutes, then remove from the water.

Peel the skin off the kidneys and cut in half horizontally. Remove the cores (middles) and slice the kidneys.

Put the bacon in a non-stick pan (skillet) and heat gently until the fat begins to run out, then increase the heat, add the onions and kidneys and fry quickly to brown. Lift out with a slotted spoon and place on a warm plate.

Stir the flour into the fat remaining in the bottom of the pan (skillet) and cook for a minute. Gradually blend in the wine and the stock and bring to the boil, stirring until thickened. Blend in the tomato purée and seasoning, then return the kidneys, onions and bacon to the pan (skillet).

Cover and simmer gently for about 20 minutes until the kidneys are tender. Taste and adjust seasoning before serving.

Serves 4

VEGETABLES IN VARIETY

In a healthy diet, vegetables must play a major part, and at least two meals per week should be meat-free. Vegetables contain dietary fibre, vegetable proteins and varied vitamins and minerals – all vital for general health. I think in the following pages you'll find enough ideas to keep you healthily busy! For vegetables are not just second-class citizens – something to go with the centre attraction, whether it be meat, poultry or fish: they can be a special dish or course on their own, and can quite happily satisfy the hungriest appetites. For years the French have held the view that vegetables should be a course on their own; and vegetarians, of course, eat virtually nothing else. (I've created a number of recipes which are similar to the nut cutlets beloved of vegetarians – and they're delicious!) Try seeing if you can serve the family *more* vegetables by cooking them in interesting recipes. Many of those on the following pages can be served as a light lunch or supper; some are more clearly accompaniments; but try serving two or more together as an unusual and tasty meal.

The healthiest vegetables are those in peak condition, as recently plucked from the ground or plant as possible. Young vegetables are best for flavour, but as a keen, although not consistently successful, gardener, I know this is not always feasible: the last of the runner beans must be used up, or baby courgettes (zucchini) have overnight turned into marrows! But older vegetables can be used for soups, or baking in casserole dishes in the oven. When buying be very fussy about feeling, examining closely, and smelling: you only want the very best in return for your money.

When you have grown or brought your really fresh vegetables, prepare them just before cooking, and only wash or peel minimally. Most vegetable goodness is near the skin, and leaving them to soak in water leaches out many vitamins. They are really best *raw*, but this I discuss in the salad section (see page 131 onwards). Cook your fresh vegetables for as brief a time as possible in minimal water. Cover pans closely. If you have a steamer, this is the best way of cooking without losing any vitamins and minerals into the cooking liquid (Vitamin C, for instance, is lost in boiling). But be careful not to *over*-cook – steaming is a quicker process than you might think. (Improvise a steamer, by putting a metal colander over a saucepan and using foil as a lid.)

Aim to cook vegetables until just softening. All vegetables (except perhaps aubergine) should still be bright in colour, and crisp in the middle. Only cook to the soft stage if turning into a purée or a sauce (and I've included some vegetable sauces for interest and healthy flavour). Always try to use the vegetable cooking water in stocks, soups or sauces – this way you won't waste anything.

Remember, too, the basics of colour and texture. Any vegetable can be made more exciting by the addition of a topping – for instance my sesame seed crunch on page 127, a finely diced colourful vegetable like red pepper, or toasted chopped nuts or pine kernels.

Stuffed Marrow

This is a different way of serving marrow. It's a good supper dish, accompanied by a green salad. Be sure to drain it well on kitchen paper towels after blanching as marrows are rather watery (thus quite slimming!) and will thin down the sauces if not drained thoroughly.

Imperial/metric	American
1 large marrow, peeled, seeded and sliced in rings	1 large marrow, peeled, seeded and sliced in rings

Meat sauce

2 lb (900 g) lean minced beef	4 cups firmly packed ground beef
1 large onion, chopped	1 large onion, chopped
2 fat cloves of garlic, crushed	2 whole cloves of garlic, crushed
1 oz (25 g) flour	¼ cup all-purpose flour
1¾ lb (795 g) can tomatoes	3 cups canned tomatoes
2 tablespoons tomato purée	2 tablespoons tomato purée
salt and freshly ground black pepper	salt and freshly ground black pepper
4 oz (100 g) fresh brown breadcrumbs	2 cups fresh soft brown breadcrumbs

Cheese sauce

1½ oz (40 g) polyunsaturated margarine	3 tablespoons margarine
1½ oz (40 g) flour	6 tablespoons all-purpose flour
1 pint (600 ml) skimmed milk	2½ cups skim milk
8 oz (225 g) mature Cheddar cheese, grated	2 cups grated aged Cheddar cheese
1 teaspoon Dijon mustard	1 teaspoon Dijon mustard
salt and freshly ground black pepper	salt and freshly ground black pepper

Blanch the slices of marrow in boiling water for a minute then cool under running cold water. Drain very thoroughly on kitchen paper towels. Arrange in the bottom of a large roasting tin.

For the meat sauce, put the mince (ground beef) in a non-stick saucepan and heat gently until the fat begins to run out, then increase heat and fry until browned. Add onion and garlic and cook for a few more minutes to brown the onion. Stir in flour, then add tomatoes, purée, salt and pepper and bring to the boil, stirring until thickened. Simmer with a lid for about 30 minutes until the mince (ground beef) is tender, stirring occasionally. Remove from the heat and stir in breadcrumbs. Taste and check seasoning then spoon meat sauce into the centre of the marrow rings.

For the cheese sauce, melt the margarine in a saucepan then stir in flour and cook for a minute. Gradually blend in milk, stirring until thickened. Remove from the heat and stir in three-quarters of the cheese, mustard, salt and pepper. Pour sauce over the marrow and sprinkle with remaining cheese.

Cook uncovered in the oven at 350°F/180°C/Gas 4 for about 45 minutes until the marrow is tender. Serve straight from the oven.

Serves 6–8

Summer Vegetables in Mild Curry Sauce

A good and tasty non-meat meal, to be served with boiled brown rice to sop up the sauce. Any mixture of vegetables can be used, depending on what is in season.

Imperial/metric	American
1½ oz (40 g) polyunsaturated margarine	3 tablespoons margarine
1 medium onion, sliced	1 medium onion, sliced
3 sticks celery, sliced	3 stalks celery, sliced
3 courgettes, sliced	3 zucchini, sliced
4 oz (100 g) button mushrooms, sliced	1 cup sliced button mushrooms
4 tomatoes	4 tomatoes
salt and freshly ground black pepper	salt and freshly ground black pepper

Sauce	Sauce
1 level teaspoon curry powder	1 level teaspoon curry powder
1 oz (25 g) flour	¼ cup all-purpose flour
½ pint (300 ml) good stock, cooled	1¼ cups good stock, cooled
¼ pint (150 ml) skimmed milk	⅔ cup skim milk
2 teaspoons redcurrant jelly	2 teaspoons redcurrant jelly
salt and freshly ground black pepper	salt and freshly ground black pepper

Heat the margarine in a large saucepan and quickly fry onion and celery until soft. Add courgettes (zucchini) and continue to fry until courgettes (zucchini) are just beginning to soften, then add mushrooms. Cook for a minute then transfer vegetable mixture to a shallow ovenproof dish with a slotted spoon. Skin the tomatoes then slice them and arrange on top of the vegetables. Season well with salt and pepper.

For the sauce, put the curry powder and flour in a saucepan, then *very* gradually blend in the stock with a wire whisk. Bring to the boil, stirring until thickened. Stir in the milk, redcurrant jelly and seasoning. Heat until the sauce just reaches boiling point, then pour over vegetables.

Cook in the oven at 350°F/180°C/Gas 4 for about 30 minutes until vegetables are heated through and the sauce is bubbling.

Serves 3

Vegetable Casserole

Serve this tomato casserole hot, with well flavoured grated Cheddar cheese sprinkled on top to add to the protein content. It can be served as a supper dish, or as a vegetable accompaniment.

Imperial/metric	American
2 tablespoons sunflower oil	2 tablespoons sunflower oil
1 large onion, chopped	1 large onion, chopped
3 sticks celery, chopped	3 stalks celery, chopped
3 carrots, sliced	3 carrots, sliced
14 oz (397 g) can tomatoes	1½ cups canned tomatoes
2 tablespoons tomato purée	2 tablespoons tomato purée
½ pint (300 ml) good stock	1¼ cups good stock
15 oz (425 g) can red kidney beans, drained	1½ cups canned red kidney beans, drained
salt and freshly ground black pepper	salt and freshly ground black pepper
1 small cauliflower, broken into small florets	1 small cauliflower, broken into small florets
4 oz (100 g) button mushrooms	1 cup button mushrooms

Heat the oil in a saucepan and quickly fry onion, celery and carrot until beginning to brown. Stir in tomatoes, purée, stock, beans and seasoning. Cover with a lid and simmer for about 20 minutes until the carrot is just tender then add the cauliflower and mushrooms and cook for a further 5 minutes.

Serves 4

Broccoli and Cauliflower Polonaise

Be sure not to overcook the vegetables as they soon begin to lose their goodness. Both should still be fairly crisp when served. Serve as a light main dish or as an accompanying vegetable.

Imperial/metric	American
12 oz (350 g) cauliflower, broken into florets	12 oz cauliflower, broken into florets
12 oz (350 g) broccoli spears	12 oz broccoli spears
1½ oz (40 g) polyunsaturated margarine	3 tablespoons margarine
1 oz (25 g) fresh brown breadcrumbs	½ cup fresh soft brown breadcrumbs
1 tablespoon freshly chopped parsley	1 tablespoon freshly chopped parsley
1 hard-boiled egg	1 hard-cooked egg

Cook the cauliflower and broccoli in boiling salted water for about 4 minutes, so that they are still crisp in the centre. Drain thoroughly, arrange on a warm serving dish, and keep warm.

Melt the fat in a saucepan, add the breadcrumbs and fry quickly for about 2 minutes until golden brown. Remove from the heat, stir in the parsley and spoon over cauliflower and broccoli.

Garnish with the egg, which can either be chopped or sliced.

Serves 4

Cheesy Leeks
with Bacon

This dish makes a light meal in itself. If you like, serve with crisp French bread.

Imperial/metric	American
4 medium leeks	4 medium sized leeks
8 rashers lean bacon, lightly grilled	8 Canadian bacon slices, lightly broiled
Sauce	Sauce
1 oz (25 g) butter	2 tablespoons butter
½ oz (15 g) flour	2 tablespoons all-purpose flour
½ pint (300 ml) skimmed milk	1¼ cups skim milk
3 oz (75 g) mature Cheddar cheese, grated	¾ cup grated aged Cheddar cheese
1 teaspoon Dijon mustard	1 teaspoon Dijon mustard
salt and freshly ground black pepper	salt and freshly ground black pepper
fresh parsley to garnish	fresh parsley to garnish

Cut the coarse green leaves off the leeks. Cut a deep slit through all the green and half the white part of the leeks and open up. Wash thoroughly under running cold water. Wrap each leek in 2 rashers of bacon. Arrange in a shallow ovenproof dish so that they are just touching.

For the sauce, heat the butter in a saucepan, stir in the flour and cook for a minute. Gradually blend in the milk, and bring to the boil, stirring until thickened. Remove from the heat and add two-thirds of the cheese, the mustard and seasoning. Pour the sauce over the leeks and sprinkle with remaining cheese.

Cook uncovered in the oven at 350°F/180°C/Gas 4 for about an hour until the leeks are tender. Garnish with parsley and serve.

Serves 4

Pissaladière

This flan (pie) is a sort of cross between a quiche and a pizza. Serve hot in slices with a fresh green salad.

Imperial/metric

4 oz (100 g) self-raising flour
2 oz (50 g) plain wholewheat flour
1½ oz (40 g) lard
1½ oz (40 g) polyunsaturated margarine
about 2 tablespoons cold water

Filling

2 tablespoons sunflower oil
2 onions, sliced
14 oz (397 g) can peeled tomatoes
2 fat cloves of garlic, crushed
2 tablespoons tomato purée
1 teaspoon light muscovado sugar
2 tablespoons freshly chopped parsley
salt and freshly ground black pepper
4 oz (100 g) well flavoured Cheddar cheese, grated
1¾ oz (45 g) can anchovy fillets, drained

American

1 cup self-rising flour
½ cup wholewheat flour
3 tablespoons shortening
3 tablespoons margarine
about 2 tablespoons cold water

Filling

2 tablespoons sunflower oil
2 onions, sliced
1½ cups canned tomatoes
2 fat cloves of garlic, crushed
2 tablespoons tomato purée
1 teaspoon light brown sugar
2 tablespoons freshly chopped parsley
salt and freshly ground black pepper
1 cup grated aged Cheddar cheese
1¾ oz can anchovy fillets, drained

Heat the oven to 425°F/220°C/Gas 7. Put a baking tray (cookie sheet) in the oven to heat through.

Measure the flours into a bowl and rub in fats until mixture resembles fine breadcrumbs. Bind together with water to form a stiff dough, then turn out onto a lightly floured surface and knead until smooth. Roll out and use to line an 8 inch (20 cm) flan tin (pie pan). Chill in the refrigerator for 15 minutes, then bake blind for about 20 minutes. Remove the greaseproof paper (non-stick parchment) and baking beans for the last 10 minutes to dry out the base of the flan (pie shell).

For the filling, heat the oil in a pan, then fry the onions for about 10 minutes until brown. Add the tomatoes, garlic, tomato purée, sugar, parsley and seasoning and simmer without a lid until thick and pulpy (about 10 minutes). Sprinkle the cheese over the base of the flan (pie shell) and pour the tomato mixture on top. Arrange the anchovy fillets in a lattice pattern on top of the tomato.

Reduce the oven heat to 375°F/190°C/Gas 5 and cook flan on the hot baking sheet (cookie sheet) for about 25 minutes until the filling is hot and bubbling.

Serves 4–6

Courgette and Green Pepper Quiche

This is a very colourful quiche and a good way of using courgettes (zucchini) if you have an abundance of them in the garden and don't want to serve them as an accompanying vegetable. Serve warm in slices with a salad for a light lunch or supper.

Imperial/metric	American
6 oz (175 g) self-raising flour	1½ cups self-rising flour
2 oz (50 g) wholewheat flour	½ cup wholewheat flour
2 oz (50 g) lard	¼ cup shortening
2 oz (50 g) polyunsaturated margarine	¼ cup margarine
about 2 tablespoons cold water	about 2 tablespoons cold water

Filling

1 oz (25 g) polyunsaturated margarine	2 tablespoons margarine
8 oz (225 g) courgettes, sliced	8 oz zucchini, sliced
1 green pepper, seeded and chopped	1 green pepper, seeded and chopped
3 oz (75 g) well flavoured Cheddar cheese, grated	⅓ cup grated aged Cheddar cheese
3 eggs, beaten	3 eggs, beaten
¼ pint (150 ml) skimmed milk	⅔ cup skim milk
salt and freshly ground black pepper	salt and freshly ground black pepper

Heat the oven to 400°F/200°C/Gas 6. Put a baking tray (cookie sheet) in the oven to heat through.

Measure the flours into a bowl and rub in fats until mixture resembles fine breadcrumbs. Bind together with water, then turn out onto a lightly floured surface. Knead gently until smooth and chill in the refrigerator if time allows. Roll out and use to line a 9 inch (22.5 cm) loose-bottomed flan tin (pie pan). Chill in the refrigerator for about 30 minutes.

For the filling, heat the margarine in a saucepan and fry courgettes (zucchini) for about 5 minutes until beginning to soften, then add green pepper. Cook for a few more minutes until courgettes (zucchini) are beginning to brown and pepper is beginning to soften. Sprinkle the cheese over the bottom of the flan case (pie shell) and spoon courgettes (zucchini) and pepper on top. Blend the eggs with the milk and seasoning, and pour into flan case (pie shell).

Cook in the oven on the baking tray (cookie tray) for 15 minutes then reduce the oven temperature to 350°F/180°C/Gas 4 for about 25 minutes until pastry is cooked and filling has set.

Serves 6

Baked Parsnip with Cheesy Topping

If you do not have enough ham for this recipe, bacon pieces work just as well. Serve parsnips straight from the oven with fresh granary bread.

Imperial/metric

a little sunflower oil
1 lb (450 g) parsnips
8 oz (225 g) ham, chopped
8 oz (225 g) can tomatoes
1 tablespoon freshly chopped
  parsley
salt and freshly ground black
  pepper
2 oz (50 g) fresh brown
  breadcrumbs
2 oz (50 g) mature Cheddar
  cheese, grated
a little Parmesan cheese

American

a little sunflower oil
1 lb parsnips
1 cup chopped smoked ham
¾ cup canned tomatoes
1 tablespoon freshly chopped
  parsley
salt and freshly ground black
  pepper
1 cup fresh soft brown
  breadcrumbs
½ cup grated aged Cheddar
  cheese
a little Parmesan cheese

Heat the oven to 350°F/180°C/Gas 4. Lightly oil a 2 pint/1.2 litre (5 cup) ovenproof dish.

Peel the parsnips and roughly chop, removing the hard core in the middle. Mix with the ham and turn into the prepared dish. Pour the tomatoes on top, sprinkle with parsley, and season well with salt and pepper.

Mix the breadcrumbs and cheeses together in a bowl, then sprinkle over the parsnips. Bake in the oven for about 45 minutes until the parsnips are tender and the topping is crisp.

Serves 4

Crispy Bacon and Potato Pie

This is a good lunch dish. Serve with green salad.

Imperial/metric

2 lb (900 g) potatoes, peeled
  and boiled until tender
1 oz (25 g) polyunsaturated
  margarine
a little skimmed milk
salt and freshly ground black
  pepper
6 oz (175 g) mature Cheddar
  cheese, grated
8 oz (225 g) bacon pieces,
  chopped
1 onion, chopped
2 tablespoons freshly chopped
  chives
tomato and watercress to
  garnish

American

2 lb potatoes, peeled and boiled
  until tender
2 tablespoons margarine
a little skim milk
salt and freshly ground black
  pepper
1½ cups grated aged Cheddar
  cheese
1 cup chopped bacon
1 onion, chopped
2 tablespoons freshly chopped
  chives
tomato and watercress to
  garnish

Heat the oven to 400°F/200°C/Gas 6. Mash the well-drained potatoes with the margarine, a little milk and seasoning, then mix in two-thirds of the cheese. Put the bacon pieces in a non-stick pan (skillet) and heat gently until the fat begins to run out. Increase heat, add onion, and fry until bacon is crispy and onion is tender.

Spread one-third of the potato in the bottom of a lightly greased shallow 2 pint/1.2 litre (5 cup) ovenproof dish. Mix the chives with the bacon and spread half of this over the potato. Repeat with another layer of potato and then bacon and spoon the remaining potato on top. Sprinkle with remaining cheese.

Cook for about 20 minutes until the cheese is bubbling and beginning to brown. Serve garnished with slices of tomato and sprigs of watercress.

Serves 4

Mushroom Soufflé

I like to cook soufflés in shallow dishes as then everyone gets more of the crispy topping. The eggs and cheese are good (if not served too often), and it makes a light family lunch or supper.

Imperial/metric	American
1 oz (25 g) polyunsaturated margarine	2 tablespoons margarine
8 oz (225 g) button mushrooms, sliced	2 cups sliced button mushrooms
1 oz (25 g) flour	¼ cup all-purpose flour
½ pint (300 ml) skimmed milk	1¼ cups skim milk
4 eggs, separated	4 eggs, separated
salt and freshly ground black pepper	salt and freshly ground black pepper
1 tablespoon freshly chopped parsley	1 tablespoon freshly chopped parsley
1 oz (25 g) Cheddar cheese, grated	¼ cup grated Cheddar cheese
1 oz (25 g) fresh brown breadcrumbs	½ cup fresh soft brown breadcrumbs

Heat the oven to 375°F/190°C/Gas 5. Lightly grease a 2 pint/1.2 litre (5 cup) shallow ovenproof dish.

Heat the margarine in a saucepan and fry mushrooms for about 5 minutes until tender. Stir in flour and cook for a minute then gradually blend in milk. Bring to the boil, stirring until thickened, then remove from the heat and stir in egg yolks, seasoning and parsley.

Whisk the egg whites in a bowl with an electric or rotary whisk until they form soft peaks. Fold whites into mushroom sauce until evenly blended and transfer to prepared dish. Mix the cheese and breadcrumbs and sprinkle over top of soufflé.

Cook in the oven for about 25 minutes until well risen and a golden brown. Serve straight from the oven with a green salad.

Serves 4

Mushroom Burgers

Rather than beefburgers, serve these to vegetarians – they are quite delicious and do make a change. Serve hot with a green vegetable or salad.

Imperial/metric

8 oz (225 g) onion, very finely chopped

8 oz (225 g) open mushrooms, finely chopped

8 oz (225 g) mature Cheddar cheese, grated

8 oz (225 g) fresh brown breadcrumbs

2 tablespoons freshly chopped parsley

salt and freshly ground black pepper

2 eggs, beaten

a little wholewheat flour

about 1½ oz (40 g) polyunsaturated margarine

American

2 cups finely chopped onion

2 cups chopped mushrooms

2 cups grated aged Cheddar cheese

4 cups soft fresh brown breadcrumbs

2 tablespoons freshly chopped parsley

salt and freshly ground black pepper

2 eggs, beaten

a little wholewheat flour

3 tablespoons margarine

Cook the chopped onion in boiling salted water for about 5 minutes until tender, then drain well and put in a bowl with the mushrooms, cheese, breadcrumbs, parsley and seasoning. Bind the mixture together with the eggs, mixing thoroughly so that the ingredients are evenly blended.

Divide the mixture into twelve equal portions then with lightly floured hands shape into burgers. Arrange on a plate, cover with clingfilm (plastic wrap) and chill in the refrigerator for about 6 hours before cooking.

When required, heat the margarine in a non-stick pan (skillet) and cook burgers for about 20 minutes, turning once during cooking until cooked through and golden brown on both sides.

Serves 6

Pasta in Leek and Mushroom Sauce

This dish can be served as a 'vegetable' accompaniment, or as a meal in itself, accompanied by a fresh green salad. Try to use wholewheat pasta wherever possible, as it contains so much more healthy goodness.

Imperial/metric

8 oz (225 g) pasta shells or
  bows
1½ oz (40 g) polyunsaturated
  margarine
2 leeks, washed and sliced
6 oz (175 g) open mushrooms,
  sliced
1 oz (25 g) flour
½ pint (300 ml) chicken stock
¼ pint (150 ml) skimmed milk
salt and freshly ground black
  pepper
4 oz (100 g) well flavoured
  mature Cheddar cheese

American

2 cups pasta shells or bows
3 tablespoons margarine
2 leeks, washed and sliced
1½ cups sliced mushrooms
¼ cup all-purpose flour
1¼ cups chicken stock
⅜ cup skim milk
salt and freshly ground black
  pepper
1 cup grated aged Cheddar
  cheese

Cook the pasta in boiling salted water as directed on the packet. Drain and rinse well with running cold water.

Heat the margarine in a saucepan and fry leeks for about 10 minutes until tender, then add mushrooms and cook for a further few minutes. Stir in flour and cook for a minute then gradually blend in stock and milk. Bring to the boil, stirring until thickened. Remove from heat, stir in pasta and season to taste.

Turn into a 2 pint/1.2 litre (5 cup) ovenproof dish, sprinkle with cheese then cook in the oven at 375°F/190°C/Gas 5 for about 15–20 minutes until cheese has melted and is bubbling, and the pasta has heated through.

Serves 3 as a main course

Apple and Nut Loaf

A good 'meat' dish for a vegetarian – and quite delicious, too. Serve accompanied by a green salad.

Imperial/metric	American
4 oz (100 g) dry roast peanuts	¾ cup dry roast peanuts
4 oz (100 g) shelled cashew nuts	¾ cup shelled cashew nuts
2 oz (50 g) polyunsaturated margarine	¼ cup margarine
1 onion, chopped	1 onion, chopped
2 tomatoes, skinned and roughly chopped	2 tomatoes, skinned and roughly chopped
2 Cox's apples, peeled, cored and diced	2 dessert apples, peeled, cored and diced
1 oz (25 g) rolled oats	¼ cup rolled oats
2 tablespoons freshly chopped parsley	2 tablespoons freshly chopped parsley
salt and freshly ground black pepper	salt and freshly ground black pepper
1 egg, beaten	1 egg, beaten
a little skimmed milk	a little skim milk
sliced tomato and parsley to garnish	sliced tomato and parsley to garnish

Heat the oven to 350°F/180°C/Gas 4. Lightly grease a 1 lb (450 g) loaf tin (loaf pan).

Chop the nuts, reserving eight of the cashews for garnish. Heat the margarine in a saucepan, add onion, tomato and apple, and fry for about 5 minutes until soft. Stir in the chopped nuts, oats, parsley and seasoning. Bind together with the egg and enough milk to give a fairly moist consistency.

Press the mixture into the loaf tin (loaf pan), cover with a piece of lightly greased foil, and bake in the oven for about an hour until firm. Remove the foil for the last 15 minutes of cooking time. Turn out onto a warm serving dish and garnish with reserved nuts, parsley and tomato.

Serves 4

Crunchy Walnut Burgers

These burgers are perfect for a vegetarian but I find they are popular with meat eaters too! Serve with a fresh green salad.

Imperial/metric	American
1 tablespoon sunflower oil	1 tablespoon sunflower oil
1 small onion, finely chopped	1 small onion, finely chopped
4 oz (100 g) walnuts and peanuts mixed, chopped	1 cup mixed walnuts and peanuts, chopped
1½ oz (40 g) rolled oats	¼ cup rolled oats
1 egg, beaten	1 egg, beaten
2 tablespoons skimmed milk	2 tablespoons skim milk
salt and freshly ground black pepper	salt and freshly ground black pepper
a little oil for frying	a little oil for frying

Heat the oil in a saucepan, fry onion for about 5 minutes until soft, then stir in the nuts and oats and mix well. Add the egg and milk and season well.

Divide the mixture in half and with lightly floured hands shape into a ball and then flatten to form a burger. Chill in the refrigerator for about 6 hours.

Heat a little oil in a frying pan (skillet) and fry the burgers for about 3 minutes on each side until brown and crisp on the outside.

Serves 2

Mediterranean Aubergines

Good to make in late summer when both aubergines and tomatoes are at their best. Serve with poultry or fish dishes.

Imperial/metric	American
¾–1 lb (350–450 g) aubergines	¾–1 lb aubergines
salt and freshly ground black pepper	salt and freshly ground black pepper
8 oz (225 g) tomatoes	8 oz tomatoes
sunflower oil	sunflower oil
1 tablespoon freshly chopped parsley	1 tablespoon freshly chopped parsley

Slice the aubergines and cook in boiling salted water for 5 minutes, then drain thoroughly on kitchen paper. Skin the tomatoes then slice.

Lightly oil a shallow ovenproof dish and layer the aubergines and tomatoes in the dish, seasoning well between each layer. Sprinkle with the parsley and cover the dish with foil. Cook in the oven at 375°F/ 190°C/Gas 5 for about 40 minutes until the aubergines are tender.

Serves 4–6

Three Beans in Garlic Butter

A really colourful combination. The red kidney beans will need to be soaked overnight before they are cooked, and they must be boiled for at least 10 minutes, longer obviously than the others.

Imperial/metric	American
8 oz (225 g) baby broad beans	1 cup fava beans
8 oz (225 g) runner beans, sliced	1 cup snap beans, sliced
8 oz (225 g) red kidney beans, soaked overnight	1 cup dried red kidney beans, soaked overnight
2 oz (50 g) butter	¼ cup butter
1 clove of garlic, crushed (or more to taste)	1 clove of garlic, crushed (or more to taste)

Cook each of the beans separately in boiling salted water until just tender, and then drain well. Mix together. Blend the butter and garlic then heat in a saucepan. Add the beans and cook for about 3 minutes until evenly coated in butter and heated through. Turn into a serving dish and serve straightaway.

Serves 6

Cabbage and Bacon

It is best to use young fresh cabbage for this recipe, and the stir-frying method, although in oil, keeps in many of the cabbage nutrients, as well as retaining the crispness.

Imperial/metric	American
1 small white cabbage	1 small white cabbage
1 tablespoon sunflower oil	1 tablespoon sunflower oil
4 oz (100 g) bacon pieces, roughly chopped	½ cup chopped bacon

Finely shred the cabbage, removing any tatty outside leaves.

Heat the oil in a large saucepan and gently fry bacon pieces until the fat runs out. Increase heat and fry quickly until crisp. Add the cabbage and continue to cook over a high heat for about 5 minutes, tossing the cabbage all the time. Serve straightaway.

Serves about 4

Sweet and Sour Red Cabbage

This is the best way of serving red cabbage I know, it really is good. Delicious with grilled or roast meat, especially pork.

Imperial/metric

12 oz (350 g) red cabbage
1 lb (450 g) Bramley apples
¼ pint (150 ml) water
1½ oz (40 g) light muscovado
  sugar
salt
4 cloves
6 tablespoons white wine
  vinegar
1 oz (25 g) polyunsaturated
  margarine
1 tablespoon redcurrant jelly

American

12 oz red cabbage
1 lb cooking apples
⅔ cup water
3 tablespoons tightly packed
  light brown sugar
salt
4 cloves
6 tablespoons white wine
  vinegar
2 tablespoons margarine
1 tablespoon redcurrant jelly

Shred cabbage finely and peel, core and slice apples. Put all the ingredients together in a saucepan. Bring to the boil then cover saucepan with a lid and simmer gently for about 45 minutes, stirring occasionally, until the cabbage is tender.

Taste and check seasoning, remove cloves, and serve hot.

Serves 4

Honeyed Carrots

Carrots are particularly nice served this way, and they're full of goodness, particularly Vitamin A. The honey gives the carrots a lovely flavour. If you want to, you can peel the carrots, but much of the flavour and vitamin content is in the skin.

Imperial/metric

1 lb (450 g) carrots, well
   scrubbed and sliced
1 oz (25 g) butter
1 tablespoon runny honey
freshly chopped parsley

American

1 lb carrots, well scrubbed and
   sliced
2 tablespoons butter
1 tablespoon liquid honey
freshly chopped parsley

Cook the carrots in boiling salted water for about 10 minutes until barely tender. Drain well. Heat the butter and honey together in a saucepan, then add the carrots. Cook and stir for a couple of minutes until evenly coated with honey, then turn into a serving dish and sprinkle with freshly chopped parsley.

Serves 4

in oven
with stew

Braised Celery

This is a useful recipe to make when you can get inexpensive trimmed celery heads at the supermarket (they are usually past their best for eating with cheese). Serve hot with roast meat or oven-baked chops.

Imperial/metric	American
1 head celery	*1 head celery*
1 lb (450 g) onions, sliced	*1 lb onions, sliced*
salt and freshly ground black pepper	*salt and freshly ground black pepper*
1 pint (600 ml) good light stock	*2½ cups good light stock*
freshly chopped parsley to garnish	*freshly chopped parsley to garnish*

Heat the oven to 350°F/180°C/Gas 4.

Wash the celery well and cut into 3 inch (7.5 cm) lengths. Arrange the celery in layers with the onion in a 3 pint/1.75 litre (7½ cup) ovenproof dish. Season with salt and pepper and pour over stock.

Cover dish with a lid or piece of foil and cook in the oven for about 1½ hours until the celery is tender. Sprinkle with freshly chopped parsley.

Serves 6

Courgettes (Zucchini) with Parsley

Courgettes (zucchini) are one of my favourite vegetables – full of taste and goodness – and this is a good way of serving them, to accompany any grilled (broiled) meat or chicken dish.

Imperial/metric

1 lb (450 g) courgettes
2 oz (50 g) polyunsaturated
  margarine
salt and freshly ground black
  pepper
2 tablespoons freshly chopped
  parsley

American

1 lb zucchini
¼ cup margarine
salt and freshly ground black
  pepper
2 tablespoons freshly chopped
  parsley

Rinse and wipe the courgettes (zucchini), and cut into ⅛ inch (3 mm) slices.

Heat the fat in a pan (skillet), add the courgettes (zucchini) with seasoning, and fry briskly for about 5 minutes until the courgettes (zucchini) are a pale golden brown. Sprinkle with the parsley and turn into a warm serving dish.

Serves 4

Peas and Courgettes (Zucchini)

As an alternative to courgettes (zucchini) serve peas with mange-tout on a special occasion. This idea spins out either courgettes or mange-tout which are expensive out of season.

Imperial/metric	American
8 oz (225 g) courgettes	8 oz zucchini
12 oz (350 g) frozen peas, thawed	2¼ cups frozen peas, thawed
knob of butter	knob butter

Top and tail the courgettes (zucchini), and then either cut into slices or, if large, dice them. Put into a saucepan of boiling salted water with the peas. Cover saucepan with a lid and simmer gently for about 5 minutes or until just tender. Drain thoroughly. Return to the saucepan and toss in butter over a gentle heat.

Serves 4

Courgettes with Tomato and Prawn (Shrimp) Sauce

Serve this dish either as a light lunch or as a starter with a little salad.

Imperial/metric	American
2 good sized courgettes	2 good sized zucchini
1 oz (25 g) polyunsaturated margarine	2 tablespoons margarine
1 small onion, chopped	1 small onion, chopped
1 oz (25 g) flour	2 tablespoons all-purpose flour
¾ pint (450 ml) skimmed milk	2 cups skim milk
1 tablespoon tomato purée	1 tablespoon tomato purée
salt and freshly ground black pepper	salt and freshly ground black pepper
4 oz (100 g) peeled prawns	½ cup shelled shrimp
2 oz (50 g) mature Cheddar cheese, grated	½ cup grated aged Cheddar cheese
1 oz (25 g) fresh brown breadcrumbs	½ cup fresh soft brown bread crumbs

Heat the oven to 350°F/180°C/Gas 4.

Cut the courgettes (zucchini) in half lengthwise and scoop out and discard seeds from middle. Cook in a saucepan of boiling salted water for about 5–8 minutes until just tender. Drain well on kitchen paper towels and arrange in a shallow ovenproof dish so that they are just touching.

Heat the margarine in a saucepan and fry onion for about 5 minutes until soft and then stir in flour. Cook for a minute then gradually blend in the milk, and bring to the boil, stirring until thickened. Stir in purée, seasoning and prawns (shrimp), then spoon over courgettes (zucchini). Mix cheese and breadcrumbs together and sprinkle over sauce.

Cook in the oven for about 40 minutes until the sauce is bubbling and cheese and breadcrumbs are a golden brown.

Serves 4

Courgette (Zucchini), Onion and Tomato Casserole

This is a good way of using up larger courgettes (zucchini), and there's no need to add stock as they cook in their own juices. Serve with grilled pork chops or sausages.

Imperial/metric	American
4 large courgettes	*4 large zucchini*
4 tomatoes	*4 tomatoes*
1 small onion	*1 small onion*
a little butter	*a little butter*
salt and freshly ground black pepper	*salt and freshly ground black pepper*

Slice the courgettes (zucchini), skin and slice the tomatoes, and finely chop the onion.

Lightly butter an ovenproof casserole and put the courgettes (zucchini), tomatoes and onion in alternate layers in the dish. Season well. Dot with a little butter, cover with a piece of foil and cook in the oven at 350°F/180°/Gas 4 for about 40 minutes until the courgettes (zucchini) are tender.

Serves 4

Peas and Onions in Yogurt Sauce

This is a rather unusual vegetable dish, delicious when served with cold sliced meats such as tongue or turkey.

Imperial/metric

1 lb (450 g) fresh shelled peas
8 oz (225 g) pickling onions,
  peeled, topped and tailed
1 oz (25 g) polyunsaturated
  margarine
1 oz (25 g) flour
¼ pint (150 ml) natural yogurt
  (see page 17)
salt and freshly ground black
  pepper

American

3 cups shelled peas
8 oz baby onions, peeled,
  topped and tailed
2 tablespoons margarine
¼ cup all-purpose flour
⅔ cup unflavored yogurt (see
  page 17)
salt and freshly ground black
  pepper

Cook the peas and onions separately in boiling salted water until just tender. Drain both vegetables, reserving ½ pint/300 ml (1¼ cups) of the onion water for the sauce. Keep the vegetables warm.

To make the sauce, heat the margarine in a saucepan, stir in flour and cook for a minute. Gradually blend in onion liquid, bring to the boil, stirring until thickened. Remove from the heat, then stir in yogurt and seasoning. Fold in the cooked vegetables. Transfer to a warmed serving dish to serve.

Serves 4–6

Foil-Baked Onion

Cook each onion, one per person, in a piece of foil alongside baked potatoes. Both are healthy – the onion full of goodness, and the baked potato lacking none of the vitamins contained in and near the skin.

Imperial/metric	American
4 medium onions	*4 medium sized onions*
good knob of butter	*good knob of butter*
salt and freshly ground black pepper	*salt and freshly ground black pepper*
freshly chopped parsley to garnish	*freshly chopped parsley to garnish*

Heat the oven to 350°F/180°C/Gas 4.

Skin the onions and leave them whole. Stand each on a piece of foil, put a small knob of butter on top of each onion and season well with salt and pepper. Seal onion inside foil, stand in an ovenproof dish so that they are just touching, and bake in the oven for about 1½ hours until the onions are tender. (The time will vary depending on the size onions used.)

To serve, unwrap the onions and sprinkle with chopped parsley.

Serves 4

New Zealand Hedgehog Potatoes

This is a family favourite of Jackie's back home in New Zealand. By scrubbing the potatoes rather than peeling them, much more of the vitamin content is retained.

Imperial/metric	American
4 medium potatoes	*4 medium potatoes*
2 oz (50 g) butter	*¼ cup butter*
1 clove of garlic, crushed (or more to taste)	*1 clove of garlic, crushed (or more to taste)*
good pinch mixed dried herbs	*good pinch mixed dried herbs*

Scrub the potatoes clean. Make cuts about ½ inch (1.25 cm) deep across the potatoes one way and then at right angles across the other way. Mix together the butter and crushed garlic. Rub each potato generously with the butter and sprinkle with herbs.

Bake on a baking tray (cookie sheet) in the oven at 425°F/220°C/Gas 7 for about 1½ hours until the potatoes are cooked through and the skins are crisp. Serve hot with a little more garlic butter.

Serves 4

Crispy Baked Potatoes

Always a favourite to serve with salads, try different fillings with the potatoes and serve for lunch. This is really the best way of serving potatoes – skin and nutrients intact.

Imperial/metric	American
4 large potatoes	*4 large potatoes*
a little sunflower oil	*a little sunflower oil*
polyunsaturated margarine	*margarine*

Heat the oven to 400°F/200°C/Gas 6.

Scrub the potatoes well, brush with a little of the oil and bake in the oven on a baking tray (cookie tray) for about 1½ hours – the cooking time will vary with the size of the potatoes. Cut each potato in half, fork the inside and serve with a little margarine.

CHEESE AND HAM TOPPING

Scoop out the insides of the cooked potatoes, and mix with 2 oz/50 g (½ cup) well flavoured grated Cheddar cheese, 2 oz/50 g (¼ cup smoked) chopped ham and 1 teaspoon Dijon mustard. Season to taste then spoon back into potato skins and reheat in the oven for about 10 minutes.

CREAM CHEESE AND CHIVE TOPPING

Scoop out the insides of the potatoes, and mix with 3 oz/75 g (⅓ cup) cream cheese, 1 tablespoon freshly chopped chives, a crushed clove of garlic and 2 tablespoons skimmed milk. Spoon back into the potato skins and reheat for about 10 minutes.

TOMATO AND ONION TOPPING

Scoop out the middle of the potatoes, and mix with 2 chopped skinned tomatoes and 2 oz/50 g (½ cup) fried onion. Season to taste then spoon back into potato skins and reheat in the oven for about 10 minutes.

Serves 4

French Vegetable Purées

These are very popular now, but be sure to include texture in another part of the meal (crisp rolls or perhaps croûtons with the soup, for instance), and don't have a soft pudding as well! For special occasions serve three different purées grouped together in one vegetable dish: choose contrasting colours such as the following. You can introduce texture to these as well by sprinkling with some of my sesame seed crunch, for instance (page 127), or merely toasted seeds of some kind, or pure kernels.

CELERIAC PURÉE

Cook equal quantities of celeriac and potato until tender in boiling salted water. Drain well then mash to a purée. Season to taste with salt and freshly ground black pepper, and serve with a knob of butter on top.

SPROUT PURÉE

Cook the sprouts in boiling salted water. Drain well then transfer to a processor or blender and reduce to a purée with 2 tablespoons skimmed milk, salt and freshly ground black pepper. Heat a little butter in the bottom of a saucepan and reheat purée before serving.

SWEDE PURÉE

Cook the swede in boiling salted water until tender. Drain well then mash with a potato masher until smooth. Season well with salt and freshly ground black pepper, and stir in a little skimmed milk to give more smoothness. Serve with a knob of butter on top.

Almondy Rice

A good and healthy meat accompaniment, but it's also good for vegetarians.

Imperial/metric	American
3 tablespoons sunflower oil	3 tablespoons sunflower oil
1 red pepper, seeded and diced	1 red pepper, seeded and diced
6 spring onions, chopped	6 scallions, chopped
8 oz (225 g) brown rice	1 cup brown rice
1 pint (600 ml) good stock	2½ cups good stock
salt and freshly ground black pepper	salt and freshly ground black pepper
1 tablespoon freshly chopped parsley	1 tablespoon freshly chopped parsley
4 oz (100 g) mushrooms, sliced	1 cup sliced button mushrooms
4 oz (100 g) flaked almonds	1 cup flaked almonds
4 hard-boiled eggs	4 hard-cooked eggs

Heat the oil in a large saucepan and fry pepper and onions for about 5 minutes. Add rice and cook gently until all the oil has been absorbed. Add the stock, seasoning and parsley, bring to the boil, cover with a lid and simmer gently for about 30 minutes, stirring occasionally to prevent the mixture from sticking.

Add the mushrooms and cook for about 10 more minutes until the rice is tender and all the stock has been absorbed.

Remove from the heat, stir in the almonds, and turn into a warm serving dish. Quarter the eggs and arrange on top, sprinkle with a little more freshly chopped parsley, and serve straightaway.

Serves 4

Sesame Seed Crunch

Sesame seeds and sunflower seeds, often thought to be 'crank' vegetarian fare, are actually very good indeed for everyone. They contain many vitamins (particularly Vitamin E) and minerals, and as well as *tasting* good, they're good for the skin and hair as well as general health. Wonderful over a salad, over vegetables or rice. I am really addicted to this marvellous mixture.

Imperial/metric	American
4 oz (100 g) sesame seeds	*1 cup sesame seeds*
8 oz (225 g) sunflower seeds	*2 cups sunflower seeds*
knob of butter	*knob of butter*
1 tablespoon sunflower oil	*1 tablespoon sunflower oil*
8 oz (225 g) flaked almonds	*2 cups flaked almonds*

Put seeds in a dry non-stick saucepan, cover with a lid and dry roast over a medium heat for about 5 minutes, tossing all the time. (Keep the lid on otherwise the seeds will pop all over the kitchen floor!)

Melt the butter in another pan, add oil and almonds and cook until browned all over. Stir in the seeds and use as a topping when you want to add crunch and flavour. Store in a jar in the fridge and use as required.

Summer Spinach Sauce

This sauce is good with cold chicken or as a dressing for a pasta salad. Spinach, of course, as every Popeye fan knows, is very good for you, containing plenty of iron.

Imperial/metric

8 oz (225 g) fresh leaf spinach, chopped

salt and freshly ground black pepper

a little grated nutmeg

¼ pint (150 ml) whole egg mayonnaise (see page 132)

American

3 cups chopped raw leaf spinach

salt and freshly ground black pepper

a little grated nutmeg

⅔ cup whole egg mayonnaise (see page 132)

Wash spinach thoroughly and place in a saucepan with about 4 tablespoons water and a little salt. Bring to the boil, tossing with a wooden spoon to prevent it sticking. Cover and simmer for about 4 minutes until tender, then add pepper and nutmeg. Reduce to a purée in a processor or blender.

Allow to cool then stir into the mayonnaise in a bowl. Taste and check seasoning before serving.

Serves 4

Onion and Watercress Sauce

The potato simply thickens this sauce. It is especially good with grilled (broiled) cod or haddock, decorated with the best leaves from the watercress (which is a good source of sulphur and iodine).

Imperial/metric	American
knob of butter	*1 tablespoon butter*
1 tablespoon sunflower oil	*1 tablespoon sunflower oil*
1 large onion, finely chopped	*1 large onion, finely chopped*
1 large potato, diced	*1 large potato, diced*
1 bunch watercress	*1 bunch watercress*
¼ pint (150 ml) chicken stock	*⅔ cup chicken stock*
salt and freshly ground black pepper	*salt and freshly ground black pepper*
a little grated nutmeg	*a little grated nutmeg*
a little plain yogurt or single cream, if liked	*a little unflavored yogurt or light cream, if liked*

Heat butter and oil in a non-stick saucepan and sauté the onion and potato with the lid on, tossing from time to time for about 10 minutes. Add roughly chopped watercress (save the best leaves for garnish). Add stock and seasonings and simmer gently until the potato and onion are tender and the mixture is a thickish pulp. Reduce to a purée in a processor or blender.

Return to the saucepan and reheat until piping hot and serve with a little yogurt or cream stirred in if liked.

Serves 4

Real Tomato Sauce

Nothing is quite like real, fresh, home-made tomato sauce, for health and taste. Serve with fish, grilled meat or poultry.

I quite like the seeds left in, but you can sieve them out if you like. Make the sauce when you have really ripe tomatoes or perhaps when there is a glut at the end of the summer (it freezes well).

Imperial/metric	American
2 lb (900 g) ripe tomatoes	2 lb ripe tomatoes
good knob of butter	1 tablespoon butter
8 oz (225 g) onions, roughly chopped	2 cups chopped onion
1 fat clove of garlic, crushed	1 whole clove of garlic, crushed
a few leaves marjoram, chopped	a few leaves marjoram, chopped
1 teaspoon light muscovado sugar	1 teaspoon light brown sugar
¼ pint (150 ml) chicken stock	⅔ cup chicken stock
salt and freshly ground black pepper	salt and freshly ground black pepper

Nick the skin of the tomatoes with a sharp knife, then dip them into boiling water for a few moments. The skins will now slip off easily.

In a large non-stick saucepan, melt the butter, then add onions and garlic. Cover with a lid and cook over a low heat for 20 minutes, shaking the saucepan from time to time until the onions are tender. Add tomatoes, marjoram, sugar and stock. Mash tomatoes down and allow to boil until reduced to a thickish pulp. Season to taste then reduce to a purée in a processor or blender. Reheat in the saucepan until piping hot.

Serves 4–6

ENJOYING
OUR SALAD DAYS

When you realise how much of the goodness of vegetables is leached away into the cooking liquid, you can appreciate the worth of raw salads! Eating vegetables raw means no goodness is lost: they retain their full dietary fibre, vitamin and mineral content. As before though, the vegetables must be in peak condition. Try to use all vegetables as soon as you can: they deteriorate with storage.

One of my most successful party dishes ever was based on treating a wide range of vegetables as if they were salads. I used an old Victorian meat platter, and on it I arranged groups of prepared salad vegetables in neat triangular piles, leaving a space in the centre for a bowl containing a 'dip'. I used a home-made whole egg mayonnaise (see page 132, and for a pretty variation, add a mashed avocado and extra lemon juice). The vegetables were strips of yellow, green and red pepper, sprigs of cauliflower, tiny button mushrooms, radishes, cherry tomatoes, chicory leaves and some celery and carrot cut into sticks, as well as cucumber boats (peel a cucumber, cut in half lengthways, scoop out seeds with a teaspoon and cut in chunks for boats).

Most of the salads in this section use raw vegetables; a few, which are more substantial – to be served for a light summer lunch, say – include cooked ingredients (I recommend particularly the hot chicken salad). Dressed salads as accompaniments go very well with rice, meat, fish and poultry dishes when you are not serving a sauce.

Never just confine salads to the summer months – winter vegetables make wonderfully crunchy and tasty salads, and their raw goodness is particularly needed in the cold of winter. And remember that even the simplest lettuce salad can be transformed by sprinkling with something interesting texturally – like my sesame seed crunch (see page 127).

Whole Egg Mayonnaise

Using a processor or blender, this mayonnaise is really quick and easy to prepare.

Imperial/metric	American
2 eggs	2 eggs
2 tablespoons white wine vinegar	2 tablespoons white wine vinegar
1 teaspoon caster sugar	1 teaspoon caster sugar
1 teaspoon dry mustard	1 teaspoon dry mustard
salt and freshly ground black pepper	salt and freshly ground black pepper
about 1 pint (600 ml) sunflower oil	about 2½ cups sunflower oil
juice of 1 lemon	juice of 1 lemon

Put all the ingredients except the oil in a processor or blender. Switch on to a low speed to blend. Add the oil in a slow steady stream with the mixer on fast speed, until the mixture is very thick and all the oil has been absorbed.

Add lemon juice, process until mixed then taste and check seasoning.

Makes about 1½ pints/900 ml (2¾ cups)

FRESH HERB MAYONNAISE

To ½ pint/300 ml (1¼ cups) mayonnaise, add 2 tablespoons double (heavy) cream and 2 tablespoons freshly chopped herbs.

CURRIED MAYONNAISE

To ½ pint/300 ml (1¼ cups) mayonnaise, add ½ teaspoon curry powder and 1 tablespoon mango chutney sauce.

GARLIC MAYONNAISE

To ½ pint/300 ml (1¼ cups) mayonnaise, add 2 crushed cloves of garlic.

Yogurt Dressing

Any variety of salads can be tossed in this dressing, which is rather lighter than mayonnaise.

Imperial/metric

4 tablespoons mayonnaise (see
 page 132)
4 tablespoons natural yogurt
4 tablespoons soured cream
4 tablespoons white wine
 vinegar
salt and freshly ground black
 pepper

American

4 tablespoons mayonnaise (see
 page 132)
4 tablespoons unflavored yogurt
4 tablespoons soured cream
4 tablespoons white wine
 vinegar
salt and freshly ground black
 pepper

Blend all the ingredients together in a bowl with some seasoning. Chill in the refrigerator covered with clingfilm (plastic wrap) before serving.

Makes about ½ pint/300 ml (1¼ cups)

French Dressing

This dressing is particularly nice for tossing a green salad, but is good with rice and mixed salads too.

Imperial/metric

¼ pint (150 ml) sunflower oil
1 small clove of garlic, crushed
½ teaspoon dry mustard powder
salt and freshly ground black
  pepper
1 teaspoon caster sugar
about 6 tablespoons white wine
  vinegar

American

⅔ cup sunflower oil
1 whole clove of garlic, crushed
½ teaspoon dry mustard
salt and freshly ground black
  pepper
1 teaspoon caster sugar
about 6 tablespoons white wine
  vinegar

Blend the oil with the garlic, mustard, seasoning and sugar, then stir in the vinegar. Taste and adjust seasoning if necessary. It stores well in a screw-top jar in the refrigerator.

Makes ½ pint/300 ml (1¼ cups) dressing

Low Calorie Dressing

When watching calories, this is perfect for cheering up a salad. Ideal if you want to keep fat down in the diet.

Imperial/metric	American
1 teaspoon Dijon mustard	*1 teaspoon Dijon mustard*
1 tablespoon lemon juice	*1 tablespoon lemon juice*
1 tablespoon white wine vinegar	*1 tablespoon white wine vinegar*
1 clove of garlic, crushed	*1 clove of garlic, crushed*
5 oz (150 g) natural yogurt (see page 17)	*½ cup unflavored yogurt (see page 17)*
salt and freshly ground black pepper	*salt and freshly ground black pepper*

Blend all the ingredients together and season to taste. Keep in a covered bowl in the refrigerator for up to 10 days.

LOW CALORIE MINT DRESSING

Add a heaped teaspoon of freshly chopped mint to the basic recipe and mix well. This is a delicious dressing for new potatoes (although *they're* not so slimming)!

Makes a scant ½ pint/300 ml (1¼ cups)

Turkey and Rice Salad

Assemble this main-course salad well ahead and keep in the refrigerator, which gives the flavours a chance to develop.

Imperial/metric	American
1½ lb (675 g) cold cooked turkey, diced	3 cups cold cooked turkey, diced
8 oz (225 g) brown rice	1 cup brown rice
8 oz (225 g) fresh pineapple, chopped	1 cup chopped fresh pineapple
2 oz (50 g) sultanas	¼ cup seedless white raisins
2 tablespoons freshly chopped chives	2 tablespoons freshly chopped chives
4 oz (100 g) button mushrooms	1 cup button mushrooms
2 oz (50 g) cashew nuts	½ cup cashew nuts
1 small red pepper, cored, seeded and chopped	1 small red pepper, cored, seeded and chopped
1 small yellow pepper, cored, seeded and chopped	1 small yellow pepper, cored, seeded and chopped
¼ pint (150 ml) French dressing (see page 134)	⅔ cup French dressing (see page 134)

Put the cold turkey in a bowl. Cook the rice in plenty of boiling salted water as directed on the packet. Drain thoroughly, rinse in running cold water, then drain again. Add to the turkey along with the pineapple, sultanas and chives. Pour boiling water over the mushrooms and leave to stand for 5 minutes then drain and slice finely. Add to the rice mixture with the cashew nuts and peppers. Add the dressing and mix well until thoroughly blended.

Cover with clingfilm (plastic wrap) and store in the refrigerator for several hours before serving.

To serve, taste and check seasoning, then pile into a serving dish.

Serves 6

Chicken and Avocado Salad

Serve this for a nutritious lunch in the summer. Chicken, avocado and mayonnaise – with the tang of horseradish – are cool and satisfying.

Imperial/metric	American
2 ripe avocado pears	2 ripe avocado pears
lemon juice	lemon juice
2 tablespoons apple juice	2 tablespoons apple juice
2 tablespoons horseradish sauce	2 tablespoons horseradish sauce
2 tablespoons good thick mayonnaise (see page 132)	2 tablespoons good thick mayonnaise (see page 132)
salt and freshly ground black pepper	salt and freshly ground black pepper
6 baby beetroots, sliced	6 baby beetroots, sliced
8 slices cold cooked chicken breast	8 slices cold cooked chicken breast
watercress to garnish	watercress to garnish

Peel the avocado pears, cut in half, remove stones and roughly chop. Toss in lemon juice to prevent them discolouring.

Blend the apple juice, horseradish sauce and mayonnaise together in a bowl and season to taste. Stir in the avocado. Arrange the beetroot and chicken around a flat dish and spoon the avocado mixture in the middle. Garnish with sprigs of watercress.

Serves 4

Hot Chicken Salad

Perfect for a lunch party on a hot summer's day. Serve with warm brown rolls.

Imperial/metric

1 small curly endive or ½ a
  medium one
a few leaves of lamb's lettuce
a little watercress
a few radicchio leaves
½ green pepper, seeded
4 oz (100 g) mild streaky
  bacon, snipped into fine strips
3 oz (75 g) flaked almonds
salt and freshly ground black
  pepper
4 raw chicken breasts, cut into ½
  inch (1.25 cm) strips
6 tablespoons French dressing
  (see page 134)
a little freshly chopped parsley

American

1 small curly endive or ½ a
  medium one
a few leaves of lamb's lettuce
a little watercress
a few radicchio leaves
½ green pepper, seeded
1 cup chopped bacon
⅔ cup flaked almonds
salt and freshly ground black
  pepper
4 raw chicken breasts cut into ½
  inch strips
6 tablespoons French dressing
  (see page 134)
a little freshly chopped parsley

Prepare all the salad leaves, cutting the endive and other type of lettuce into manageable pieces. Finely slice the pepper.

Put the bacon in a non-stick frying pan (skillet) and cook slowly until fat begins to run out. Increase heat and fry until nearly crispy, then add almonds and allow to brown. Lift out of pan (skillet) with a slotted spoon. Season chicken and quickly cook for about 5 minutes, tossing to brown on all sides. Return bacon and almonds to pan for a moment.

Toss the salad ingredients in the dressing, and divide between four plates. Top with the warm chicken mixture, sprinkle with parsley, and serve immediately.

Serves 4

Avocado and Prawn Salad

I like to serve this salad with a natural yogurt dressing (see page 133).

Imperial/metric	American
2 ripe avocado pears	2 ripe avocado pears
lemon juice	lemon juice
1 iceberg lettuce	1 iceberg lettuce
1 lb (450 g) peeled prawns	2⅔ cups shelled shrimp
¼ cucumber, sliced	¼ cucumber, sliced
8 radishes, sliced	8 red radishes, sliced
1 lemon, sliced	1 lemon, sliced

Peel the avocado pears, cut in half, remove and discard the stones. Slice the avocado and toss in a little lemon juice to prevent them from discolouring.

Tear the outer leaves from the lettuce and use to line a serving dish. Cut the lettuce heart into wedges and arrange on the serving dish with the peeled prawns (shelled shrimp) and the slices of cucumber, radish and lemon. Serve with natural yogurt dressing (see page 133).

Serves 4

Green Bean, Tomato and Liver Salad

I find it best to use fresh rather than frozen chicken livers for this recipe. It makes a good iron-rich light lunch.

Imperial/metric	American
8 oz (225 g) chicken livers	*8 oz chicken liver*
1 tablespoon sunflower oil	*1 tablespoon sunflower oil*
knob of polyunsaturated margarine	*knob of margarine*
8 oz (225 g) French beans, topped and tailed	*8 oz French beans, topped and tailed*
2 good sized tomatoes, skinned	*2 good sized tomatoes, skinned*
6 tablespoons French dressing (made with lemon juice instead of vinegar, see page 134)	*6 tablespoons French dressing (made with lemon juice instead of vinegar, see page 134)*
1 tablespoon freshly chopped chives or spring onion tops	*1 tablespoon freshly chopped chives or scallion tops*

Snip any stringy bits off the livers. Heat the oil and margarine in a pan (skillet) and fry livers for about 5 minutes, turning all the time. Cool, then cut in slim strips.

Cut each French bean in three. Cook in boiling salted water for about 4 minutes, until still crisp. Drain and allow to cool. Cut the skinned tomatoes in half, remove and discard the seeds, then cut in thin strips.

Toss livers, beans and tomatoes in French dressing then turn into a serving dish. Sprinkle with chives, and serve immediately.

Serves 4

Cheese and Apple Salad

Serve this combination of protein and Vitamin C for lunch with fresh granary rolls (ideal for a vegetarian).

Imperial/metric	American
6 sticks celery, sliced	6 stalks celery, sliced
2 Cox's apples, cored and diced	2 dessert apples, cored and diced
4 oz (100 g) blue cheese, cubed	⅔ cup blue cheese, cubed
4 oz (100 g) mature Cheddar cheese, cubed	⅔ cup diced aged Cheddar cheese
3 tablespoons sunflower oil	3 tablespoons sunflower oil
2 tablespoons good thick mayonnaise (see page 132)	2 tablespoons good thick mayonnaise (see page 132)
salt and freshly ground black pepper	salt and freshly ground black pepper
lettuce	lettuce
cucumber	cucumber

Put the celery, apple and cheese in a bowl. Mix the oil with the mayonnaise and season lightly. Pour over celery mixture and toss until evenly coated.

Arrange the lettuce on a serving dish, spoon the celery mixture into the middle, and garnish with sliced cucumber.

Serves 4

Green Salad
with Feta Cheese

This type of side-salad is served a great deal in Greece where Feta cheese traditionally comes from.

Imperial/metric	American
2 oz (50 g) black olives	½ cup black olives
1 small Cos lettuce	1 small Cos lettuce
½ cucumber, thickly sliced	½ cucumber, thickly sliced
1 small green pepper, cored, seeded and sliced	1 small green pepper, cored, seeded and sliced
1 small bunch watercress	1 small bunch watercress
4 tablespoons French dressing (see page 134)	4 tablespoons French dressing (see page 134)
4 oz (100 g) Feta cheese, cubed	1 cup cubed Feta cheese
1 tablespoon freshly chopped parsley	1 tablespoon freshly chopped parsley

Put the olives in the bottom of a salad bowl. Break the lettuce into small pieces and add to the bowl with the cucumber, pepper and watercress.

When required toss well in French dressing, arrange Feta cheese on top and sprinkle with chopped parsley.

Serves 4

Fresh Spinach Salad

Choose young fresh spinach for this salad – it's delicious and full of nutrients. A good light lunch.

Imperial/metric	American
4 oz (100 g) young spinach	4 oz young fresh spinach
2 tablespoons French dressing (see page 134)	2 tablespoons French dressing (see page 134)
2 Cox's apples	2 dessert apples
salt and freshly ground black pepper	salt and freshly ground black pepper
4 oz (100 g) mature Cheddar cheese, grated	1 cup grated aged Cheddar cheese
2 oz (50 g) button mushrooms, sliced	¼ cup sliced button mushrooms
2 sticks celery, chopped	2 stalks celery, chopped
2 hard-boiled eggs, sliced	2 hard-cooked eggs, sliced
freshly chopped parsley	freshly chopped parsley

Remove the thick centre stalk from the spinach. Wash and drain thoroughly then shred leaves finely. Toss in 1 tablespoon of the dressing. Core and slice the apples and toss in the remaining dressing.

Arrange the spinach in the bottom of a salad bowl, then a layer of apple slices on top. Season, then sprinkle on cheese. Spoon mushrooms and celery on top of cheese. Arrange eggs with rest of apple over the mushrooms and celery. Garnish with freshly chopped parsley.

Serves 3

Wholewheat Pasta Salad

A simple (and healthy) combination which is delicious when served with other salads.

Imperial/metric	American
8 oz (225 g) wholewheat pasta bows or shells	2 cups wholewheat pasta bows or shells
15 oz (425 g) can red kidney beans, drained	1 cup canned red kidney beans, drained
¼ pint (150 ml) good mayonnaise (see page 132)	⅔ cup good mayonnaise (see page 132)
1 teaspoon paprika pepper	1 teaspoon paprika pepper
salt and freshly ground black pepper	salt and freshly ground black pepper

Cook the pasta in boiling salted water for about 10 minutes or until just tender, then rinse thoroughly with hot water. Drain well and allow to cool.

Stir in the kidney beans, mayonnaise, paprika, salt and pepper. Toss well until evenly coated then turn into a large serving bowl and chill in the refrigerator for about an hour before serving.

Serves 8

Brown Rice Salad

This salad is delicious without any dressing, but you can stir in a little French dressing if you like (see page 134).

Imperial/metric	American
8 oz (225 g) brown rice	*1 cup brown rice*
15 oz (425 g) can chick peas, drained	*1½ cups canned chick peas, drained*
4 oz (100 g) sultanas	*½ cup seedless white raisins*
2 oz (50 g) walnut pieces	*½ cup walnut pieces*
1 large stick celery, chopped	*1 large stalk celery, chopped*
salt and freshly ground black pepper	*salt and freshly ground black pepper*

Cook the rice in boiling salted water as directed on the packet. (Remember that brown rice does take longer to cook than ordinary long-grain rice.) Rinse well under running cold water, drain, and allow to cool.

Stir in the chick peas, sultanas, walnuts, celery and seasoning to taste. Turn into a serving dish and chill for a couple of hours in the refrigerator before serving.

Serves about 8

Iceberg Salad

This is a light salad, a perfect accompaniment to cold meats. Once dressed the lettuce will begin to go limp so toss in dressing just before serving.

Imperial/metric

1 small iceberg lettuce
3 sticks celery, sliced
1 Cox's apple, cored and sliced
juice of ½ lemon
4 oz (100 g) seedless green grapes
1 oz (25 g) walnuts, chopped
4 tablespoons French dressing (see page 134)
a few black grapes to garnish

American

1 small iceberg lettuce
3 stalks celery, sliced
1 dessert apple, cored and sliced
juice of ½ lemon
1 cup seedless green grapes
¼ cup chopped walnuts
4 tablespoons French dressing (see page 134)
a few black grapes to garnish

Shred the lettuce, arrange in the bottom of a salad bowl, then add the celery. Dip the apple in lemon juice to prevent the slices from discolouring, and add to the lettuce with the green grapes and walnuts.

Just before serving, pour on the dressing, toss well until evenly coated, then garnish with black grapes.

Serves 6

Swiss Salad

This is a wonderfully coloured and textured salad to serve on more special occasions – all the colours of green from light to dark, with the glowing red of the radicchio.

Imperial/metric	American
1 iceberg lettuce	*1 iceberg lettuce*
a few heads lamb's lettuce	*a few heads lamb's lettuce*
1 curly endive, sliced	*1 curly endive, sliced*
a few radicchio leaves	*a few radicchio leaves*
1 tablespoon freshly chopped dill	*1 tablespoon freshly chopped dill*
4 tablespoons French dressing (see page 134)	*4 tablespoons French dressing (see page 134)*

Break the lettuce leaves into small pieces in the salad bowl. Add the lamb's lettuce, sliced curly endive and the radicchio leaves with the dill.

Just before serving add French dressing and toss well.

Serves 6

Mushroom Salad

I prefer to leave the mushrooms whole for this salad, but if you are only able to get larger button mushrooms, then slice them.

Imperial/metric

¼ pint (150 ml) water
4 tablespoons sunflower oil
salt and freshly ground black
  pepper
½ teaspoon ground coriander
12 oz (350 g) small button
  mushrooms
4 fl. oz (100 ml) Madeira
2 sticks celery, chopped

American

⅔ cup water
4 tablespoons sunflower oil
salt and freshly ground black
  pepper
½ teaspoon ground coriander
3 cups small button mushrooms
½ cup Madeira
2 stalks celery, chopped

Put the water, oil, seasoning, coriander and whole mushrooms in a saucepan. Bring to the boil and simmer gently, without a lid, for about 5 minutes. Lift the mushrooms out of the pan with a slotted spoon and put in a bowl. Add the Madeira to the liquid left in the saucepan, and boil rapidly until liquid has reduced to a syrup. Pour over the mushrooms.

Allow to cool, then cover with clingfilm and chill in the refrigerator overnight. Just before serving, stir in the celery, then transfer salad to a serving dish.

Serves 6

Tomato Salad

Make this salad in late summer when tomatoes are at their most plentiful and cheapest. A French dressing made with a little walnut oil (if you can afford it!) is delicious, and fresh spicy basil could be used instead of the chives.

Imperial/metric

1 lb (450 g) firm tomatoes
1 small onion, finely sliced
4 tablespoons French dressing
  (see page 134)
salt and freshly ground black
  pepper
1 tablespoon freshly chopped
  chives

American

1 lb firm tomatoes
1 small onion, finely sliced
4 tablespoons French dressing
  (see page 134)
salt and freshly ground black
  pepper
1 tablespoon freshly chopped
  chives

Slice the tomatoes and arrange in a shallow serving dish in neat layers. Arrange the onion slices on top of the tomato, pour over French dressing and season well with salt and pepper. Chill well and just before serving sprinkle with chives.

Serves 4

Cucumber and Dill in Mayonnaise

Both dill and cucumber are perfect for serving with cold fish such as trout and, on very special occasions, salmon. Have all the ingredients chilled before you start preparing.

Imperial/metric	American
½ pint (300 ml) good thick mayonnaise (see page 132)	1¼ cups good thick mayonnaise (see page 132)
½ cucumber	½ cucumber
1 tablespoon freshly chopped dill	1 tablespoon freshly chopped dill
salt and freshly ground black pepper	salt and freshly ground black pepper

Measure the mayonnaise into a bowl. Peel the cucumber and cut into small cubes. Mix into the mayonnaise with the dill, and season to taste with salt and pepper. Serve straightaway.

Serves 6

CUCUMBER AND FRESH DILL SALAD

Peel a cucumber with a potato peeler, then cut into very thin slices and arrange on a serving dish. Pour ¼ pint/150 ml (⅔ cup) French dressing (see page 134) over cucumber, and season with freshly ground white pepper. Cover with clingfilm (plastic wrap) and chill in the refrigerator until required. Just before serving, sprinkle with chopped fresh dill.

Multi Bean Salad

Bean salads are not just healthy: I find they are always popular amongst friends; and they don't take too long to prepare. Just remember the beans do need soaking overnight first.

Imperial/metric	American
4 oz (100 g) flageolet beans	½ cup flageolet beans
4 oz (100 g) butter beans	¾ cup butter beans
4 oz (100 g) aduki beans	½ cup aduki beans
4 oz (100 g) red kidney beans	¾ cup red kidney beans
1 fat clove of garlic, crushed	1 whole clove of garlic, crushed
3 spring onions, chopped	3 scallions, chopped
4 sticks celery, chopped	4 stalks celery, chopped
4 tablespoons French dressing (see page 134)	4 tablespoons French dressing (see page 134)
a little freshly chopped parsley	a little freshly chopped parsley

Put the beans in separate bowls and leave to soak overnight. Drain well, then cook separately as directed by the manufacturers on the side of the packets. Drain well, allow to cool.

Mix beans together in a bowl with the remaining ingredients. Turn into a serving dish and sprinkle with a little chopped parsley before serving.

Serves 6

Winter Vegetable Salad

This salad is good to make during the winter months when fresh salad ingredients are a bit more expensive and less readily available.

Imperial/metric	American
2 medium carrots, diced	2 medium sized carrots, diced
1 small turnip, diced	1 small turnip, diced
4 oz (100 g) French beans, chopped	½ cup chopped French beans
3 tablespoons French dressing (see page 134)	3 tablespoons French dressing (see page 134)
2 medium potatoes, washed	2 medium sized potatoes, washed
¼ pint (150 ml) good mayonnaise (see page 132)	⅔ cup good mayonnaise (see page 132)
1 hard-boiled egg	1 hard-cooked egg
1 tablespoon freshly chopped parsley	1 tablespoon freshly chopped parsley

Cook the carrots, turnip and beans in boiling salted water until barely tender, then drain well and toss in French dressing whilst still warm.

Cook the potatoes in their skins in boiling salted water until tender. Cool, then remove skins, and dice.

Add, when cold, to the other vegetables with the mayonnaise. Mix well then turn into a serving dish.

Quarter the egg and use to garnish the salad, along with the chopped parsley.

Serves 6

152

Curried Coleslaw

This salad goes very well with cold meats and makes a nice change from the usual coleslaw.

Imperial/metric

3 tablespoons good mayonnaise (see page 132)
3 tablespoons French dressing (see page 134)
½ teaspoon Dijon mustard
½ teaspoon curry powder
2 teaspoons mango chutney sauce
2 Cox's apples, peeled, cored and chopped
6 oz (175 g) seedless green grapes
15 oz (425 g) can pineapple chunks in natural juice, drained
8 oz (225 g) white cabbage, shredded

American

3 tablespoons good mayonnaise (see page 132)
3 tablespoons French dressing (see page 134)
½ teaspoon Dijon mustard
½ teaspoon curry powder
2 teaspoons mango chutney sauce
2 dessert apples, peeled, cored and chopped
1½ cups seedless green grapes
1 cup canned pineapple, drained
8 oz white cabbage, shredded

Mix the mayonnaise, French dressing, mustard, curry powder and chutney sauce together in a large bowl. Add the remaining ingredients and mix well.

Turn into a glass serving dish, cover with clingfilm (plastic wrap), and chill well in the refrigerator before serving to give the flavours a chance to develop.

Serves 6

WHAT'S FOR PUDDING?

This is a section in which I expect you will think I am going to say sternly 'no puddings'. What a negative approach that would be – and how hard on family meal times! Of course, if you've followed my advice in earlier sections, and have served both a good filling and nutritious starter and main course, the family may not have *room* for a pudding! But puddings still remain a favourite with many, so I have tried to create recipes which are traditional in flavour and cooking method, but which cut down on certain less happy ingredients, add others, and still taste delicious!

Use some wholewheat flour in a crumble topping, and in the pastry for a fruit pie, for added goodness. It gives a lovely nutty flavour. And when making fruit pies add variety by mixing blander fruits with stronger ones. I often mix rhubarb with any of the soft berry fruits – it helps to spin them out – and I think even less confident gardeners always have an abundance of rhubarb. (We do anyway!) Apples, too, are very versatile, so mix them with other fruits. Cut down on the sugar content of many of the recipes, if you like, to taste, or try honey instead.

Whenever possible, though, I serve fresh, raw fruit to the family. For one thing this saves such an enormous amount of time that I am free to bake, or make first courses, and so on. Again it is important to provide plenty of variety. Take the time to arrange the bowl or platter of fruit attractively. An interesting fruit bowl will have a choice of three or four items – apples, oranges and bananas – plus some seasonal fruits. There is an abundance of soft citrus fruit during the winter months and satsumas are very popular. Include plums and pears, or cherries and grapes, snipped into sections, during their seasons. With such a choice, the family will not miss a 'proper' pudding, and with so many health-conscious people around nowadays, I have found that serving fresh fruit at a dinner party has become immensely popular. My fresh fruit extravaganza (page 165) really is stunning.

Never forget either, the food value and versatility of yogurt. I gave a recipe for home-made yogurt in the breakfast section (see page 17), and this can be used as a pudding in a variety of ways: mix it with fresh fruit for your own health-packed fruit yogurt (commercial varieties contain a *lot* of sugar); use it as a base for fools instead of cream or custard; use it to pad out cream in cake or sponge fillings; and use it *instead* of cream as a topping.

Apple Charlotte

Use old rather than very fresh bread for this, it is easier to manage.

Imperial/metric

1½ lb (675 g) cooking apples,
   peeled, cored and sliced
2 tablespoons water
4 oz (100 g) honey
1 egg, separated
4 oz (100 g) polyunsaturated
   margarine
a little caster sugar
6 slices brown bread

American

1½ lb cooking apples peeled,
   cored and sliced
2 tablespoons water
½ cup honey
1 egg, separated
½ cup margarine
a little sugar
6 slices brown bread

Put the apple in a saucepan with the water. Cook covered with a lid until soft, then remove from the heat and stir in the honey and egg yolk. Beat well. Heat the oven to 400°F/200°C/Gas 6.

Melt the margarine in a saucepan and use some to oil the sides of a 6 inch (15 cm) round cake tin or soufflé dish (cake pan), then sprinkle with a little caster sugar so that the tin (cake pan) is completely coated.

Remove the crusts from the bread, leaving two slices whole, and cut the remainder into 1½ inch (3.75 cm) wide strips. Dip strips in the melted margarine and press around the sides of the tin (cake pan), leaving no gaps. Put one whole dipped slice on the base of the tin (cake pan). Lightly beat the egg white and brush over the joins. Spoon in the apple purée. Dip the remaining slice of bread in margarine and cover the top of the apple with it. Trim the sides so that the charlotte is level.

Bake in the oven for about 20 minutes, then reduce the oven to 375°F/190°C/Gas 5 and bake for a further 40 minutes until the bread is golden brown and crisp. Run a knife around the charlotte, turn out and serve with natural yogurt.

Serves 6

Blackberry and Apple Pudding

This is a very filling pudding, ideal when you've a hungry family to feed. Serve hot with some natural (unflavoured) yogurt on top.

Imperial/metric

4 oz (100 g) self-raising flour
4 oz (100 g) wholemeal flour
2 teaspoons baking powder
4 oz (100 g) shredded suet
¼ pint (150 ml) water

Filling

1½ lb (675 g) Bramley cooking apples, peeled, cored and sliced
12 oz (350 g) blackberries
about 4 oz (100 g) golden granulated sugar

American

1 cup self-rising flour
1 cup wholewheat flour
2 teaspoons baking powder
¾ cup shredded suet
⅔ cup water

Filling

1½ lb cooking apples, peeled, cored and sliced
3 cups blackberries
½ cup sugar

Lightly grease a 2 pint/1.2 litre (5 cup) pudding basin.

Measure the flours and baking powder into a bowl, stir in the suet and mix to a soft dough with the water. Turn out onto a lightly floured surface and knead gently until smooth. Roll out two-thirds of the pastry and use to line the prepared basin.

Arrange the apples and blackberries in layers with the sugar in the basin. Roll out the remaining pastry to form the lid, moisten edges of pastry with water and lift lid on top. Secure edges well. Cover with a lid of greaseproof paper (non-stick parchment) and then foil, both pleated to allow for expansion.

Steam or boil, over or in a pan of boiling water, for about 1½ hours, topping up with water as necessary, until the pastry is cooked. Turn out of basin and serve immediately.

Serves 6–8

Loganberry and Apple Crumble

If you have a stock of frozen fruits in the freezer this is an excellent way of using them. Vary the fruit content with whatever you have most of, or whatever is available in the shops.

Imperial/metric	American
2 oz (50 g) plain flour	½ cup all-purpose flour
2 oz (50 g) wholemeal flour	½ cup wholewheat flour
2 oz (50 g) ground almonds	½ cup ground almonds
3 oz (75 g) polyunsaturated margarine	6 tablespoons margarine
2 oz (50 g) light muscovado sugar	⅓ cup light brown sugar
1 lb (450 g) apples, stewed and sweetened to taste with honey	1 lb apples, stewed and sweetened to taste with honey
12 oz (350 g) loganberries	3 cups loganberries
1 oz (25 g) flaked almonds	¼ cup flaked almonds

Heat the oven to 400°F/200°C/Gas 6.

Measure the flours into a bowl with the ground almonds, then rub in the margarine until the mixture resembles fine breadcrumbs. Stir in the sugar.

Mix the two fruits together in a bowl then turn into a pie dish. Spoon over crumble mixture and sprinkle with flaked almonds. Cook in the oven for about 30 minutes until the crumble and almonds are golden brown. Serve warm with a little natural (unflavored) yogurt.

Serves 6

Baked Apples

This is one of the easiest puddings to prepare and yet one of the most delicious. Choose fairly large apples.

Imperial/metric	American
4 large Bramley apples	4 large cooking apples
3 tablespoons runny honey	3 tablespoons clear honey
1 oz (25 g) almonds, chopped	¼ cup chopped almonds
2 oz (50 g) dates, chopped	⅔ cup chopped seeded dates
1 oz (25 g) sultanas	¼ cup seedless white raisins
1 oz (25 g) glacé cherries, chopped	⅛ cup candied cherries, chopped
a little butter	a little butter
a little water	a little water

Heat the oven to 350°F/180°C/Gas 4.

Rinse and wipe the apples. Remove the cores using a sharp knife or a corer, and make a slit in the skin around the centre of the apple. Arrange the apples in an ovenproof dish.

Mix the honey, almonds, dates, sultanas and cherries together in a bowl then divide between the apples, filling the core hole of each apple. Top each with a small knob of butter.

Pour a little water around the apples, just to cover the bottom of the dish, then bake in the oven for about 40 minutes until the apples are soft. Serve hot with a blob of natural (unflavored) yogurt.

Serves 4

Rhubarb Bakewell Tart

This makes a delicious pudding, served with a little natural (unflavored) yogurt on top.

Imperial/metric

4 oz (100 g) plain flour
2 oz (50 g) wholemeal flour
1½ oz (40 g) polyunsaturated margarine
1½ oz (40 g) lard
about 2 tablespoons cold water

Filling

4 oz (100 g) polyunsaturated margarine
4 oz (100 g) castor sugar
4 oz (100 g) semolina
1 egg, beaten
1 tablespoon raspberry jam
4 oz (100 g) rhubarb, roughly chopped

American

1 cup all-purpose flour
½ cup wholewheat flour
3 tablespoons margarine
3 tablespoons shortening
about 2 tablespoons cold water

Filling

½ cup margarine
½ cup sugar
⅔ cup semolina
1 egg, beaten
1 tablespoon raspberry jam
½ cup chopped rhubarb

For the pastry, measure the flours into a bowl, then rub in fats until mixture resembles fine breadcrumbs. Bind together with the water to give a stiff dough. Wrap in clingfilm (plastic wrap) and rest in the refrigerator for about 15 minutes then roll out on a lightly floured surface. Use to line an 8 inch (20 cm) flan tin (pie pan), prick the base well and return to the refrigerator. Heat the oven to 400°F/200°C/Gas 6 and put a baking sheet (cookie sheet) in it.

For the filling, measure the margarine, sugar, semolina and egg into a bowl and beat well until thoroughly blended. Spread the raspberry jam over the base of the flan (pie shell) and arrange rhubarb on top. Spoon the semolina mixture over the rhubarb and spread out evenly.

Bake in the oven on the tray (cookie sheet) for about 35 minutes until golden brown and the pastry is cooked. Leave to cool in the flan tin (pie pan) and serve cut in wedges.

Serves 8

Banana Pudding

Use ripe bananas for this pudding that you might have had in the fruit bowl a little too long.

Imperial/metric	American
6 ripe bananas	*6 ripe bananas*
2 oz (50 g) polyunsaturated margarine	*¼ cup margarine*
4 oz (100 g) light muscovado sugar	*⅔ cup light brown sugar*
3 oz (75 g) self-raising flour	*¾ cup self-rising flour*
1 oz (25 g) wholewheat flour	*¼ cup wholewheat flour*
1 egg, beaten	*1 egg, beaten*
a good pinch mixed spice	*a good pinch mixed spice*

Heat the oven to 350°F/180°C/Gas 4. Lightly grease a 2 pint/1.2 litre (5 cup) ovenproof dish.

Mash the bananas to a pulp with a fork. Melt the margarine and stir into the bananas, then add the sugar, flours, egg and mixed spice. Beat well until thoroughly blended.

Turn into the prepared dish and bake in the oven for about 45 minutes until golden brown and the pudding has shrunk slightly from the sides of the dish. Serve hot with a blob of natural unflavoured yogurt.

Serves 6

Southern Pears

The cider brings out the delicate flavour of pears.

Imperial/metric	American
1½ lb (675 g) cooking pears	*1½ lb cooking pears*
4 oz (100 g) honey	*½ cup honey*
4 cloves	*4 cloves*
½ pint (300 ml) sweet cider	*1¼ cups cider*

Peel, quarter and core the pears, then put in a saucepan with the honey, cloves and cider. Cover with a lid and simmer gently for about 30 minutes until the pears are tender. Remove and discard the cloves, turn the pears into a serving dish and serve warm with natural yogurt.

Serves 4

Fresh Fruit Fool

Use fruits that are in season. Gooseberries, raspberries, strawberries, blackcurrants, apricots and blackberries all go well in this recipe.

Imperial/metric	American
8 oz (225 g) loganberries	*2 cups loganberries*
2 tablespoons cold water	*2 tablespoons cold water*
½ pint (300 ml) natural yogurt	*1¼ cups unflavored yogurt*
about 2 tablespoons runny honey, to taste	*about 2 tablespoons liquid honey, to taste*

Put the loganberries in a saucepan with the water and cook gently for about 10 minutes until pulpy. Remove from heat and sieve, discarding seeds. This will give about ¼ pint/150 ml (⅔ cup) purée. Stir purée into the yogurt and sweeten to taste with honey. Chill well in the refrigerator before serving.

Serves 6

Apricot and Orange Fruit Purée

Apricots are particularly rich in Vitamin A, and this pudding is very refreshing. Serve in glasses with a blob of natural (unflavored) yogurt.

Imperial/metric

8 oz (225 g) dried apricots
1 pint (600 ml) carton pure orange juice
about 3 tablespoons runny honey

American

1½ cups dried apricots
2½ cups cartoned orange juice
about 3 tablespoons liquid honey

Put the apricots and orange juice in a bowl, cover with clingfilm (plastic wrap) and leave in the refrigerator overnight.

Turn the apricots and orange into a saucepan, bring to the boil, then reduce the heat and simmer gently for about 10 minutes until the apricots are tender. Turn the mixture into a processor or blender and reduce to a purée. Stir in honey to sweeten to taste, then pour into serving glasses.

Chill well before serving.

Serves 6–8

Scottish
Raspberry Mousse

Serve this mousse decorated with fresh raspberries if
you have them. A very good mousse using store-cup

Imperial/metric	American
15 oz (425 g) can raspberries in natural syrup	1 cup canned raspberries
1 packet raspberry jelly	1 packet raspberry jelly
6 oz (175 g) can evaporated milk, chilled in the refrigerator overnight	¾ cup evaporated milk, chilled in the refrigerator overnight
1 teaspoon lemon juice	1 teaspoon lemon juice
fresh raspberries, to decorate	fresh raspberries, to decorate

Strain the juice from the raspberries into a measuring jug, and make up
to ½ pint/300 ml (1¼ cups) with water. Bring the juice to the boil in a pan,
add the jelly in small pieces and stir until dissolved. Leave in a cool place
until almost set.

Sieve the canned raspberries and discard the seeds. Put the evaporated
milk and lemon juice into a bowl and beat with a rotary or small electric
whisk until it forms soft peaks. Fold the raspberry purée and evaporated
milk into the almost set jelly until thoroughly blended then turn into a
2 pint/1.2 litre (5 cup) glass serving dish and chill in the refrigerator until
required.

Just before serving decorate with a few fresh raspberries.

Serves 4

Apple and Lemon Sorbet

Serve in scoopfuls in stemmed glasses.

Imperial/metric

*1 lb (450 g) Bramley apples
(weight after peeling and
coring), sliced*
juice of 2 lemons
¼ pint (150 ml) water
*4 oz (100 g) golden granulated
sugar*
2 egg whites
sprigs of fresh mint

American

*1 lb cooking apples (weight
after peeling and coring),
sliced*
juice of 2 lemons
⅔ cup water
½ cup firmly packed sugar
2 egg whites
sprigs of fresh mint

Put the apples in a saucepan with just a little water and cook gently until soft and pulpy. Remove from the heat, stir in lemon juice, then reduce to a purée in a processor or blender. Sieve purée into a bowl.

Measure the water and sugar into a saucepan, and heat gently until sugar has dissolved. Increase heat, bring to the boil, and boil rapidly for 2 minutes. Remove from heat and leave to cool, then stir into the purée. Turn into an empty icecream container and freeze for several hours until thick and slushy. Put into a processor or blender and process for a few moments until smooth. Whisk the egg whites until stiff then fold into the apple mixture. Return to the freezer until frozen.

Serve in scoopfuls decorated with sprigs of fresh mint.

Serves 8

Fresh Fruit Extravaganza

Instead of the usual fruit salad for a party, try cutting the fruit into larger wedges or slices, and arranging on a huge platter. (Do this at the last moment, though, so that it loses none of its vitamins.) Then let everyone help themselves. No need for sugar or cream.

Imperial/metric	American
1 ripe melon	1 ripe melon
1 pineapple	1 pineapple
1 pawpaw (papaya)	1 papaya
1 mango	1 mango
2 kiwi fruit	2 kiwi
8 oz (225 g) strawberries, hulled	2 cups strawberries, hulled
3 small bunches grapes	3 small bunches grapes
a few cherries	a few cherries

Chill all fruits for several hours beforehand.

Cut melon in half, remove seeds, cut into slim wedges, and remove peel from each. Cut top off pineapple, and reserve. Slice. Cut core from slices then cut slices in half. Peel pawpaw, halve and remove seeds, then cut in wedges. Peel mango, cut wedges from the mango around the stone. Peel kiwi fruits and slice.

Arrange the fruits around the platter, keeping each type together, leaving a space in the middle for the grapes and strawberries, then place the reserved top of the pineapple at the back. Cover with clingfilm (plastic wrap) and chill until required.

Just before serving put the strawberries, cherries and grapes in the centre.

Serves 8–10

Summer Pudding

You can use any combination of red fruits, but this one works particularly well for me.

Imperial/metric	American
8 large, fairly thin slices brown bread, crusts removed	8 large fairly thin slices brown bread, crusts removed
8 oz (225 g) rhubarb	1 cup chopped rhubarb
8 oz (225 g) mixed red- and blackcurrants	¾ cup mixed red- and blackcurrants
4 oz (100 g) honey	½ cup honey
6 tablespoons water	6 tablespoons water
8 oz (225 g) small strawberries	1½ cups small strawberries
8 oz (225 g) loganberries	2 cups loganberries

Put one slice of bread to one side, and use the rest to line the bottom and sides of a 2 pint/1.2 litre (5 cup) round fairly shallow dish.

Put the rhubarb, cut in ½ inch (1.25 cm) slices, with the currants in a pan. Add the honey and water, bring to the boil then simmer gently for a few minutes until the fruit is just tender. Stir frequently to prevent it from sticking. Add the strawberries and loganberries and cook for a further minute.

Turn the mixture into the prepared dish, put the slice of bread on top, and bend over the slices around the sides towards the centre. Put a plate on top, pressing it down a little until the juices rise to the top of the dish. Leave in the refrigerator overnight, weighted down if you like.

Turn out just before serving with a blob of natural (unflavoured) yogurt.

Serves 6

Apple and Mint Fruit Salad

Fruit salad is always a popular sweet, particularly after a filling main course, and it's packed full of Vitamin C.

Imperial/metric	American
2 Granny Smith's apples	4 green dessert apples
2 Cox's Orange Pippin apples	4 red skinned dessert apples
2 Golden Delicious apples	1 cup cartoned orange juice
2 Red Delicious apples	2 tablespoons freshly chopped mint
⅓ pint (200 ml) carton pure orange juice	
2 tablespoons freshly chopped mint	

Core and dice the apples, put into a bowl, and stir into the orange juice with the mint.

Cover bowl with clingfilm (plastic wrap) and chill really well before serving. If liked serve with natural (unflavoured) yogurt or on its own.

Serves 6

Green and Gold Fruit Salad

The colour combination of this salad looks really attractive. Serve very well chilled.

Imperial/metric

15 oz (425 g) can pineapple chunks in natural juice
2 kiwi fruit, peeled and sliced
4 oz (100 g) seedless green grapes
2 pears, peeled, cored and sliced
1 mango, peeled, stoned and sliced
juice of 2 oranges
sprigs of fresh mint

American

1½ cups canned pineapple chunks
2 kiwi, peeled and sliced
4 oz seedless green grapes
2 pears, peeled, cored and sliced
1 mango, peeled, stoned and sliced
juice of 2 sweet oranges
sprigs of fresh mint

Empty the contents of the can of pineapple into a serving bowl, add the remaining fruits and mix well.

Chill well and serve in small bowls decorated with sprigs of fresh mint.

Serves 6–8

GOOD HOME BAKING

This is an important section for any parent whose children have a sweet tooth, and who is trying to cut back on the sweets they are allowed. I realise this sounds contradictory, as baking uses both fats and sugar, and the new healthy eating tries to restrict both of these! But I have been experimenting with recipes so that they retain the appeal of traditional bakes, yet keep the fat and sugar content fairly low. And of course I have used a proportion of wholewheat flour, with the extra nutritional benefits of the wheatgerm, and the higher fibre content. (Using wholewheat flour in recipes, you will find, as a general rule, that you will need to add more liquid than with white flour, as brown has a higher absorbency rate.)

I have not gone 'overboard', though, as many biscuits and cakes just would not work without the specified quantity of syrup, say; and in many recipes, the wonderful flavour that butter contributes just could not be replaced by polyunsaturated margarine.

I have started this section with delicious and nutritious granary rolls and wholewheat scones, but the general emphasis is on sweeter loaves, biscuits and cakes.

And finally, if you make these biscuits and breads at home, it is not only cheaper than buying them, but you *know* what has gone into them, thus you are avoiding another source of additives and over-refining.

Granary Rolls

Serve home-made beefburgers in these, or fill with lots of fresh salad for lunch.

Imperial/metric	American
¾ pint (450 ml) hand-hot water	2 cups hand-hot water
1 teaspoon sugar	1 teaspoon sugar
3 level teaspoons dried yeast	3 level teaspoons active dry yeast
12 oz (350 g) strong plain flour	3 cups bread flour
12 oz (350 g) granary flour	2½ cups wholewheat flour
3 teaspoons salt	3 teaspoons salt
1 tablespoon sunflower oil	1 tablespoon sunflower oil

Measure the water, sugar and yeast into a bowl, and leave to stand for about 10 minutes until a froth has formed on the surface. Put the flours and salt in a separate large bowl, make a well in the centre, and pour on the yeast liquid and the oil. Mix well until the dough leaves the sides of the bowl. Turn out on to a lightly floured surface and knead for about 10 minutes until smooth and the dough no longer sticks to the surface. Shape into a ball and put in a large polythene bag greased with a little oil. Leave for about an hour in a warm place until doubled in size.

Turn dough out onto a lightly floured surface and flatten with knuckles to knock out air. Divide into sixteen pieces and shape into rolls. Place on greased baking sheets (cookie sheets) allowing space in between to allow them to rise. Put sheets into greased polythene bags and leave until doubled in size.

Dust the rolls with a little extra granary flour and bake in the oven at 425°F/220°C/Gas 7 for about 20 minutes. The rolls will be a golden brown and sound hollow when tapped on the bottom. Allow to cool on a wire cake rack covered with a tea towel to keep them soft.

Makes 16 rolls

Wholewheat Scones

These are a nice – and healthy – change from the usual plain scones. When using wholewheat flour it is necessary to be a bit more generous with the baking powder.

Imperial/metric	American
4 oz (100 g) plain wholewheat flour	1 cup wholewheat flour
4 oz (100 g) self-raising flour	1 cup self-rising flour
1 rounded teaspoon baking powder	1 rounded teaspoon baking powder
2 oz (50 g) polyunsaturated margarine	¼ cup margarine
1 oz (25 g) light muscovado sugar	2 tablespoons firmly packed light brown sugar
2 oz (50 g) sultanas	⅓ cup seedless white raisins
1 egg	1 egg
skimmed milk	skim milk

Heat the oven to 425°F/220°C/Gas 7, and lightly grease a baking sheet.

Put the flours and baking powder in a bowl, add the margarine and rub in with the fingertips until mixture resembles fine breadcrumbs. Stir in sugar and sultanas. Crack the egg into a measuring jug and make up to a ¼ pint/150 ml (⅔ cup) with milk. Stir egg and milk into the flour and mix to a soft dough, adding a little more milk if necessary. Turn onto a lightly floured surface, knead lightly, and then roll out to ½ inch (1.25 cm) thickness.

Cut into rounds with a fluted 2½ inch (6.25 cm) cutter. Arrange scones on a baking sheet (cookie sheet), brush tops with a little milk, and bake for about 15 minutes or until a golden brown in colour. Lift the scones off the baking sheet and leave to cool on a wire cake rack.

Makes 10–12 scones

Savoury Cheese Loaf

Serve this as a snack with a piece of cheese or spread with a little (low-fat, if you like) cream cheese.

Imperial/metric

8 oz (225 g) self-raising flour
8 oz (225 g) plain wholewheat flour
1½ teaspoons baking powder
2 oz (50 g) polyunsaturated margarine
3 sticks celery, finely chopped
5 oz (150 g) mature Cheddar cheese, grated
1 fat clove of garlic, crushed
1 egg, beaten and made up to ½ pint (300 ml) with skimmed milk

American

2 cups self-rising flour
2 cups wholewheat flour
1½ teaspoons baking powder
¼ cup margarine
3 celery stalks, finely chopped
1¼ cups grated aged Cheddar cheese
1 large whole clove garlic, crushed
1 egg, beaten and made up to 1¼ cups with skim milk

Heat the oven to 350°F/180°C/Gas 4, and lightly grease and line with greaseproof paper (non-stick parchment) a 2 lb (900 g) loaf tin (loaf pan).

Put the flours and baking powder in a large bowl, then rub in the margarine until the mixture resembles fine breadcrumbs. Stir in the celery, cheese and garlic then stir in the egg and milk. Beat well for a minute until thoroughly blended.

Turn the mixture into the prepared tin (loaf pan) and bake in the oven for about 50 minutes until well risen and golden brown. A fine skewer (cake pick) will come out clean when pushed into the centre of the loaf. Allow to cool for 10 minutes in the tin (loaf pan) then turn out and remove paper (non-stick parchment). Finish cooling on a wire cake rack. Serve in slices.

Raisin Bran Bread

This is a very good teabread, and the bran content of the cereal makes it particularly valuable.

Imperial/metric	American
6 oz (175 g) raisins	1 cup raisins
4 oz (100 g) natural demerara sugar	½ cup turbinado sugar
7 oz (200 g) self-raising flour	1¾ cups self-rising flour
3 oz (75 g) All-Bran	1 cup Bran cereal
1 teaspoon baking powder	1 teaspoon baking powder
1 egg, beaten	1 egg, beaten
¼ pint (150 ml) water	⅔ cup water

Heat the oven to 325°F/160°C/Gas 3. Lightly grease and line with greaseproof paper (non-stick parchment) a 1 lb (450 g) loaf tin (pan).

Put all the dry ingredients in a bowl and bind together with the egg and water. Beat well for about 2 minutes until thoroughly mixed. Turn into prepared tin and bake in the oven for about 1½ hours until cooked. A skewer (cake pick) will come out clean when pushed into the centre of the loaf. Cool in the tin (pan) for about 5 minutes then turn out and finish cooling on a wire cake rack. Serve in slices.

Honey Fruit Loaf

Serve in slices, perfect for including in a packed lunch.

Imperial/metric	American
2 oz (50 g) currants	⅓ cup currants
8 oz (225 g) self-raising flour	2 cups self-rising flour
4 oz (100 g) wholemeal flour	1 cup wholewheat flour
1 teaspoon baking powder	1 teaspoon baking powder
3 teaspoons mixed spice	3 teaspoons mixed spice
4 oz (100 g) light muscovado sugar	½ cup light brown sugar
6 oz (175 g) runny honey	¾ cup liquid honey
1 egg, beaten	⅔ cup skim milk
¼ pint (150 ml) skimmed milk	1 egg, beaten
1 oz (25 g) demerara sugar	2 tablespoons turbinado sugar

Heat the oven to 350°F/180°C/Gas 4. Grease and line with lightly greased greaseproof paper (non-stick parchment), a 2 lb (900 g) loaf tin (loaf pan).

Measure the currants into a bowl with the flours, baking powder and mixed spice, then stir in the sugar. Add the honey, egg and milk and beat together to give a smooth dough.

Turn into the prepared tin (loaf pan), sprinkle demerara (turbinado) sugar on top, and bake in the oven for about 1¼ hours until risen and golden brown. (Test with a skewer [cake pick], which will come out clean when the loaf is done.) Allow to cool in the tin for a few minutes then turn out and finish cooling on a wire cake rack. Serve in slices.

Banana and Muesli Loaf

The muesli gives this loaf a bit of crunch and texture. I often make it if I happen to have a couple of spare bananas in the fruit bowl that are slightly over ripe.

Imperial/metric	American
8 oz (225 g) plain wholewheat flour	2 cups wholewheat flour
3 level teaspoons baking powder	3 level teaspoons baking powder
4 oz (100 g) polyunsaturated margarine	½ cup margarine
2 bananas, mashed	2 bananas, mashed
6 oz (175 g) muesli (see page 14)	1 cup breakfast muesli (see page 14)
3 oz (75 g) light muscovado sugar	6 tablespoons firmly packed light brown sugar
2 large eggs, beaten	2 large eggs, beaten
6 tablespoons skimmed milk	6 tablespoons skim milk

Heat the oven to 350°F/180°C/Gas 4. Lightly grease a 2 lb (900 g) loaf tin (loaf pan).

Measure all the ingredients into a large mixing bowl and beat well for about 2 minutes until thoroughly blended, then turn into the prepared tin (loaf pan) and level the top. Bake in the oven for about 1 hour, until well risen and golden brown. Test with a warm fine skewer (cake pick) which will come out clean if the cake is done. Allow to cool in the tin for about 5 minutes, then turn out and finish cooling on a wire cake rack.

Serve in slices with butter if liked.

Muesli Biscuits

I often have to make double the quantity of these as they disappear so quickly from the biscuit tin. The biscuits are full of grain goodness, and you can vary them according to the ingredients of your favourite muesli. A good healthy snack for children.

Imperial/metric	American
4 oz (100 g) polyunsaturated margarine	½ cup margarine
1 good tablespoon golden syrup	1 good tablespoon golden syrup
2 oz (50 g) demerara sugar	⅓ cup turbinado sugar
3 oz (75 g) muesli (see page 14)	½ cup breakfast muesli (see page 14)
3 oz (75 g) wholewheat flour	¾ cup wholewheat flour

Heat the oven to 325°F/160°C/Gas 3. Lightly grease 2 large baking sheets (cookie sheets).

Put the margarine and syrup in a small saucepan and heat gently until margarine has melted. Put the sugar, muesli and flour in a bowl then stir in melted mixture until thoroughly blended. Spoon teaspoonfuls of the mixture onto the baking sheets (cookie sheets), leaving room for them to spread.

Bake in the oven for about 20 minutes until golden brown. Allow to cool for a few minutes then lift off with a palette knife and finish cooling on a cake rack.

Makes about 20 biscuits

Crunchy Oat Squares

These are quite simple to prepare and keep well in an airtight tin.

Imperial/metric	American
5 oz (150 g) porridge oats	*1½ cups porridge oats*
4 oz (100 g) demerara sugar	*½ cup turbinado sugar*
4 oz (100 g) polyunsaturated margarine	*½ cup margarine*

Heat the oven to 375°F/190°C/Gas 5, and lightly grease a 7×11 inch (17.5×27.5 cm) shallow tin (pan).

Measure the oats and demerara (turbinado) sugar into a bowl. Melt the margarine in a small saucepan, remove from the heat and pour over the oats. Mix well until thoroughly blended, then turn into the prepared tin (cake pan) and press down to level the top.

Bake in the oven for about 20 minutes until golden brown. Mark into sixteen squares then allow to cool in the tin (pan) before lifting out with a palette knife.

Makes 16 squares

Ginger and Walnut Crunchies

Get the children to help with these biscuits – they will love to roll the mixture into balls – and they'll love to eat them too!

Imperial/metric	American
4 oz (100 g) butter	½ cup butter
2 tablespoons golden syrup	2 tablespoons golden syrup
8 oz (225 g) self-raising flour	2 cups self-rising flour
4 oz (100 g) wholemeal flour	1 cup wholewheat flour
2 teaspoons ground ginger	2 teaspoons ground ginger
1 teaspoon bicarbonate of soda	1 teaspoon bicarbonate of soda
6 oz (175 g) golden granulated sugar	¾ cup firmly packed sugar
2 oz (50 g) walnuts, chopped	½ cup chopped walnuts
1 egg, lightly beaten	1 egg, lightly beaten

Heat the oven to 300°F/150°C/Gas 2. Lightly grease 2 to 3 large baking trays (cookie sheets).

Measure the butter and syrup into a pan and heat gently until the butter has melted. Measure the flours, ginger, bicarbonate of soda, sugar and walnuts into a bowl and bind together with the melted butter and beaten egg.

Cool slightly until cool enough to handle then take teaspoonfuls of the mixture, roll into balls and arrange on baking sheets (cookie sheets), leaving a little room for them to spread. Bake in the oven for about 30 minutes until golden brown.

Cool on the trays (cookie sheets) for a minute then lift off with a palette knife and finish cooling on a wire cake rack. Store in an airtight tin.

Makes about 35 crunchies

Apple Shortcake

Peel and slice the apples straight onto the shortcake mixture. This stops them from discolouring if it is then baked straightaway.

Imperial/metric	American
1 oz (25 g) plain wholewheat flour	¼ cup wholewheat flour
3 oz (75 g) self-raising flour	¾ cup self-rising flour
2 oz (50 g) butter	¼ cup butter
1 oz (25 g) caster sugar	2 tablespoons firmly packed sugar
1 medium Bramley apple	1 medium sized cooking apple
1 dessertspoon demerara sugar	1 dessertspoon turbinado sugar

Heat the oven to 350°F/180°C/Gas 4.

Put the flours in a bowl and rub in butter until mixture resembles fine breadcrumbs. Reserve about a tablespoon of this mixture for the topping. Mix the caster sugar into the rest and press into the bottom of a 7 inch (17.5 cm) square tin (cake pan). Peel, core and slice the apple, and arrange slices on top of the shortcake. Mix the demerara sugar with the reserved topping and sprinkle over the apple.

Bake in the oven for about 20 minutes until the apple is tender. Divide into nine squares while still warm, then allow to cool in the tin before lifting out.

Makes 9 squares

Special Gingerbread

Try not to be tempted to eat the gingerbread straightaway as it does improve with keeping.

Imperial/metric	American
6 oz (175 g) self-raising flour	1½ cups self-rising flour
6 oz (175 g) wholemeal flour	1½ cups wholewheat flour
1 level teaspoon bicarbonate of soda	1 level teaspoon bicarbonate of soda
4 level teaspoons ground ginger	4 level teaspoons ground ginger
2 level teaspoons mixed spice	2 level teaspoons mixed spice
6 oz (175 g) polyunsaturated margarine	¾ cup margarine
12 oz (350 g) golden syrup	1½ cups golden syrup
4 oz (100 g) light muscovado sugar	⅔ cup light brown sugar
2 tablespoons marmalade	2 tablespoons marmalade
2 eggs, beaten	2 eggs, beaten
7 fl. oz (200 ml) skimmed milk	⅞ cup skim milk

Heat the oven to 325°F/160°C/Gas 3. Grease and line with lightly greased greaseproof paper (non-stick parchment) a 9×12 inch (22.5×30 cm) roasting tin (pan).

Measure all the dry ingredients into a bowl. Heat the margarine, syrup, sugar and marmalade in a saucepan until margarine has melted and sugar has dissolved. Blend together the eggs and milk then add to the dry ingredients with the syrup. Beat well for about 2 minutes until thoroughly blended.

Pour into the prepared tin and bake for about 1½ hours until golden brown (test with a fine skewer [cake pick], which will come out clean when the gingerbread is done). Allow to cool in the tin (pan), then store in an airtight tin.

Date and Cherry Fruitcake

This is a close-textured fruitcake ideal to take on picnics.

Imperial/metric	American
8 oz (225 g) plain wholewheat flour	2 cups wholewheat flour
1½ teaspoons baking powder	1½ teaspoons baking powder
½ teaspoon ground cinnamon	½ teaspoon ground cinnamon
½ teaspoon ground nutmeg	½ teaspoon ground nutmeg
4 oz (100 g) polyunsaturated margarine	½ cup margarine
3 oz (75 g) light muscovado sugar	6 tablespoons firmly packed light brown sugar
6 oz (175 g) stoned dates, chopped	1 cup chopped seeded dates
2 oz (50 g) glacé cherries, halved	½ cup candied cherries, halved
4 oz (100 g) currants	⅔ cup currants
2 eggs, beaten	2 eggs, beaten
¼ pint (150 ml) skimmed milk	⅔ cup skim milk

Heat the oven to 325°F/160°C/Gas 3. Lightly grease and line with a circle of greaseproof paper (non-stick parchment), a 7 inch (17.5 cm) round cake tin (cake pan).

Put all the ingredients in a bowl and beat well for about 2 minutes until thoroughly blended. Turn into the tin (cake pan) and level the top.

Bake in the oven for an hour and then reduce the temperature to 275°F/140°C/Gas 1 for about a further 30 minutes until the cake is cooked. (A warm skewer [cake pick] will come out clean when gently pushed into the centre of the cake.) Cool in the tin (cake pan), then turn out and peel off paper. Serve in slices.

Mini Celebration Fruit Cake

A shallow rich moist fruit cake. For those who do not like the icing on a celebration cake this is a very attractive way of decorating them.

Imperial/metric	American
8 oz (225 g) mixed dried fruit	1½ cups mixed dried fruit
4 stoned prunes, chopped	4 seeded prunes, chopped
2 tablespoons sherry	2 tablespoons sherry
grated rind and juice of 1 small orange	grated rind and juice of 1 small orange
1 oz (25 g) glacé cherries	⅛ cup candied cherries
1 oz (25 g) walnuts, chopped	¼ cup chopped walnuts
3 oz (75 g) polyunsaturated margarine	6 tablespoons margarine
2½ oz (65 g) dark muscovado sugar	⅓ cup dark brown sugar
2 oz (50 g) self-raising flour	½ cup self-rising flour
2 oz (50 g) plain wholewheat flour	½ cup wholewheat flour
1 level teaspoon mixed spice	1 level teaspoon mixed spice
2 eggs, lightly beaten	2 eggs, lightly beaten
1 level tablespoon apricot jam	1 level tablespoon apricot jam
1 level tablespoon black treacle	1 level tablespoon black treacle

Topping	Topping
apricot jam	apricot jam
glacé cherries	candied cherries
mixed nuts	mixed nuts

Measure the dried fruit and prunes into a saucepan, and pour over the sherry, orange rind and juice. Gently heat for about 5 minutes. Cover and leave in a warm place overnight. Next day add cherries and nuts to the pan.

Grease a 6 inch (15 cm) round cake tin (cake pan) and line it with lightly greased greaseproof paper (non-stick parchment).

Cream the margarine and sugar until light, fold in the flours and spice with the eggs. Beat in the jam and treacle and the mixed fruit. Turn into the tin (cake pan), level the top and bake in the oven at 275°F/140°C/Gas 1 for about 2 hours. (Test with a warm skewer [cake pick] and if it comes out clean the cake is done.)

Leave to cool in the tin (cake pan). Brush with a little apricot jam and arrange nuts and glacé cherries (candied cherries) on top and brush again with jam. This cake will keep in an airtight tin for up to 3 weeks.

DRINKING HEALTHS

The healthiest possible drink for children is plain milk, but if you can spare the time, fresh fruit drinks are well worth the effort for all the family. Many bought drinks, both 'pop' and squash, contain fruit flavouring and colouring rather than real fruit, and a lot of gas and sugar. These fill up the children so they do not want 'real' food. There's not a single good ingredient (in fact, reading the labels will horrify you). Home-made drinks are much fresher, lacking all the synthetic additives, and I am sure you will find it rewarding to see the family drinking something they enjoy while knowing it is also healthy for them.

My children actually prefer my home-made lemon squash to any of the bought drinks – even Coke! I often add one of the natural sparkling waters to a real or pure fruit juice so it has the fun of fizz. You can make nutritious milkshakes with fruit and some home-made icecream (skimmed milk for slimming adults, perhaps), and I serve cold drinks really ice cold – they taste so much better. If the glass is decorated with appropriate slices of fruit to suit the drink, plus mint sprigs, lemon balm or borage from the herb garden, it all adds to the fun.

Why health drinks? We all know that we need to have Vitamin C daily, as the body cannot store it, and a home-made fruit drink is one, pleasurable, way of supplying it. Of course, if the children – or you – eat an orange or a handful of blackcurrants each day, that will supply the necessary daily dose (or, alternatively, the squeezed juice of a fresh orange, drunk immediately).

Lemon Barley Water

A really refreshing drink, which should be served well chilled, with ice cubes.

Imperial/metric	American
4 oz (100 g) pearl barley	½ cup pearl barley
2 lemons	2 lemons
2 oz (50 g) caster sugar	¼ cup sugar
2 pints (1.2 litres) boiling water	5 cups boiling water

Put the pearl barley in a saucepan, cover with cold water and bring to the boil. Reduce the heat and simmer for about 5 minutes then drain (discard water) and put barley in a large bowl.

Peel the lemons with a potato peeler then extract the juice. Add the peel to the barley with the sugar and boiling water. Leave on one side until cold, then remove the lemon peel. Stir the lemon juice into the mixture, pour into a jug, and chill in the refrigerator until really well chilled before serving.

Serves 4

Sharp Lemon Squash

During the summer I make huge quantities of this drink and keep it in the refrigerator for when the family comes in hot and thirsty.

Imperial/metric	American
4 lemons	*4 lemons*
12 oz (350 g) caster sugar	*3 cups sugar*
1 oz (25 g) citric acid	*1 tablespoon citric acid*
2 pints (1.2 litres) boiling water	*5 cups boiling water*
sprigs of fresh mint	*sprigs of fresh mint*

Peel the lemons thinly with a potato peeler and extract juice. Put peel, sugar, citric acid and water in a bowl and stir until sugar has dissolved. Leave to become quite cold then remove lemon peel and stir in the lemon juice.

Strain into an empty clean lemonade bottle and store in the refrigerator until required. To serve, dilute the squash to taste with cold water, serve with ice cubes and sprigs of fresh mint.

Exotic Fruit Drink

Serve this well chilled on a hot summer's day. My children adore it.

Imperial/metric	American
½ Honeydew melon	*½ Honeydew melon*
½ mango	*½ mango*
½ pint (300 ml) water	*1¼ cups water*
runny honey	*liquid honey*
ice cubes	*ice cubes*

Remove and discard the seeds from the melon. Skin, dice the flesh, and put in a processor with the mango flesh and water. Reduce to a purée, taste then sweeten to taste with runny (liquid) honey. Serve in tall glasses with lots of ice cubes.

Serves 2

Spicy Cider Cup

This makes a change from serving a mulled wine at a party.

Imperial/metric

*1 litre (scant 2 pints) medium
    dry cider*
3 tablespoons runny honey
juice of ½ lemon
1 teaspoon ground nutmeg
1 stick cinnamon
apple slices to decorate

American

4¼ cups hard cider
3 tablespoons liquid honey
juice of ½ lemon
1 teaspoon ground nutmeg
1 stick cinnamon
apple slices to decorate

Measure all the ingredients (except the apple slices) into a saucepan, and heat gently. Simmer for about 10 minutes to let the flavours develop, then strain through muslin into a jug.

Serve warm decorated with slices of apple.

Serves 4–6

Malt Drink

This is always a warming drink to have before going to bed.

Imperial/metric

6 teaspoons Ovaltine
1 pint (600 ml) skimmed milk
runny honey to taste

American

*6 teaspoons powdered malt
    drink*
2½ cups skim milk
liquid honey

Add the Ovaltine (powdered malt drink) to the milk then heat in a saucepan, whisking well, until piping hot. Pour into mugs and stir in sufficient runny honey to sweeten to taste.

Serves 2

INDEX